A Guide to Rock Gardening

The Rock Gardener's Library also includes:

A Manual of Alpine and Rock Garden Plants
Edited by Christopher Grey-Wilson

Forthcoming:

The Alpine House
Robert Rolfe

Gardening with Raised Beds and Tufa
Duncan Lowe

The Propagation of Alpine Plants and Dwarf Bulbs
Brian Halliwell

Richard Bird

A Guide to Rock Gardening

CHRISTOPHER HELM

London

ISBN 0-7470-0227-4

A CIP catalogue record for this book
is available from the British Library

Typeset by Paston Press, Loddon, Norfolk
Printed and bound in Great Britain by The Bath Press

Contents

Colour plates

1. *Narcissus clusii* grown in an alpine house
2. *Cyclamen graecum* which needs the protection of an alpine house or bulb frame
3. *Ramonda myconi* growing in a shady rock crevice
4. White and purple *Fritillaria meleagris* growing in a moist spot
5. *Adonis vernalis* in a scree bed
6. A bright form of *Aubrieta deltoidea* growing in a wall
7. A newly planted stone trough
8. A strong-coloured *Primula auricula* growing in a scree bed
9. Spring in a Czechoslovakian rock garden
10. *Gypsophila cerastioides* flowering in the rock garden
11. The South African dwarf shrub *Euryops acraeus* needs a well-drained spot
12. *Genista lydia* well-suited on the top of a retaining wall
13. A well-furnished scree-bed
14. *Phlox* 'Olga' and a sempervivum on a rocky outcrop
15. The bulbous *Ipheion uniflorum* needs a sunny well-drained spot
16. *Rhodiola rosea* is a succulent that does well in the rock garden
17. *Crocus minimus* is a trouble-free bulb for the rock garden or bulb frame
18. A well-constructed rock garden
19. *Dianthus* 'Spark' is a very old cultivar
20. A colourful display of dwarf phlox spilling over a rock

Figures

1 Alpines in the Wild

Definitions

What is an alpine? That is the most difficult question in the whole of alpine gardening. Everybody knows what an alpine is but nobody can give an adequate definition. The simplest and probably the most accurate answer is: those plants grown by alpine gardeners but, unfortunately, this does not get us much farther forward.

In its truest sense alpine plants grow on the tops of mountains, above the tree-line. Put another way, they are plants which have a permanent snow-cover for part of the year. This distinction is important as many true alpines do not grow on mountains at all, but at much lower elevations, right down to sea level in some places. For example, *Saxifraga oppositifolia*, which is grown by many gardeners, thrives both in the dizzy heights of the Himalayas and in the low altitudes of the Arctic, where conditions are very similar. There are many plants that have never seen sight of a mountain that are classified as alpines: so mountains cannot be considered the sole criterion.

Alpine growers are also interested in many plants that grow further down the mountains, below the tree-line. These are often woodlanders which are more suitable for the peat garden than the rock garden. Another group of plants that most alpine gardeners grow are bulbs, many coming from low Mediterranean areas, where one of the main requisites for success is a summer baking.

So specifically we have a definition of plants that grow on the higher slopes of mountains where they get permanent snow-cover in winter or their climatically equivalent at lower altitudes. More generally they can be defined as hardy plants, usually of small stature, that need a certain degree of special treatment in the garden, i.e. they cannot simply be treated as border plants.

Let us turn the question around and ask 'What is an alpine gardener?' He is someone who provides a range of different habitats in which to grow his plants. He is not necessarily concerned with the overall effect of his plants (although many are); he is more interested in providing the right conditions for each individual plant. The plants he grows are from all parts of the world, both mountainous and lowland; they tend to be low in stature and are hardy (the use of alpine houses is not so much to exclude the cold but as protection from wet or damp weather). Some specialise in one family or genus, e.g. Primulaceae or *Saxifraga,* others grow whatever takes their fancy. In all cases it is the plant that is their prime concern. Alpine gardeners usually move into alpines from other aspects of gardening, from growing chrysanthemums or tomatoes, but, once committed, rarely move on to anything else. To grow alpines well is one of the supreme heights of gardening.

Plants in the wild

One of the fascinations of alpine gardening is that it is not just a question of following the directions on the packet. Much of the knowledge that goes into the experience of growing plants comes from observation of the plants in the wild; either from direct experience of the gardener himself, by going to the plants' native habitats or from the reading of other people's experience. Each year, either in organised parties or by themselves, many gardeners go to the mountains, from the Alps to the Himalayas and Andes, just to see how the plants grow. In former times it was also to collect plants but in this more enlightened age the plants are left for others to see, although it is still considered permissible to collect a few seeds.

These trips to the mountains have a serious side as well as providing an enjoyable holiday. In order to grow plants well, it is essential to understand how the plants grow in their natural surroundings. Much can be learnt by seeing whether a plant grows in scree or in pockets of well-drained detritus, in crevices or peaty stream sides; whether it grows in the shade or in full sun. Before causing too much concern, it should be said that you can beome a perfectly good rock gardener without getting near the mountains, but it certainly adds another dimension to gardening if you can.

One of the most noticeable features of all levels of the mountain is the snow-cover during the winter months. This is extremely important for plants; the snow acts as a protective blanket keeping the temperature from getting too cold and providing protection from the vicious winter winds. If the snow comes before the night-time temperatures get too low then the ground under the snow might be only a few degrees below freezing, even on the top of a mountain. Here plants will experience warmer conditions than they do in our gardens where the temperature can get very low, but without the benefit of the snow-cover. Another advantage of the snow is that it provides constant conditions throughout the winter. Again, in our own gardens, plants can start into growth during a particularly mild spell, only to be checked as the weather turns cold again; sometimes this cycle can happen several times during a winter. Unfortunately, although we can imitate many of the other conditions under which a plant grows, snow-cover is one which nobody has yet worked out how to achieve.

Another important aspect of the plant's life on a mountain is the amount of moisture that is available. It is often assumed that alpines never need watering but this is far from the truth. There may not be much surface water around but there is usually plenty moving down the mountain just below the surface. Two points arise from this. The first is that alpines should never be allowed to dry out completely and secondly they require good drainage to allow free passage of water; although they can cope with water passing their roots, in no way should it be allowed to become stagnant.

Like the water, air is always relentlessly on the move in the mountains and because of this alpine plants seem to resent stagnant and humid conditions. They like the protection of an alpine house but, in the main, they prefer all the windows open to keep the air circulating.

The air is thinner and purer on the mountains, so the plants get plenty of intense light. They also get more ultra-violet rays than their lowland brethren which tends to keep the plants dwarfer and more compact. In the garden alpines should be given as much light as possible. In the alpine house there is a slight problem because here light also means heat, so a compromise is reached with a certain amount of shading, but this should be removed on overcast days.

Let us now look at the various types of terrain you would be likely to see in the wild and the plants that grow in them. Starting at the lower levels as one approaches the mountain, there are the lowland meadows, often formed by clearing the forest. One of the characteristics of these meadows is that they are bursting with lush growth. The soil is full of rich humus from detritus washed down the mountain, dying vegetation and the dung from grazing animals. They are also rich in minerals and nutrients, brought down from the heights above, dissolved in snow-melt water. With all this 'washing down' there is no shortage of water.

The snow retreats earlier at the low meadow altitudes giving a longer growing season than higher up and the temperature is higher, both giving the plants an opportunity to grow larger and lusher. This wealth of nourishment means that there are a great number of species living in the meadow areas and great competition for survival. Because of the longer growing season the plants here can afford to be herbaceous, i.e. they die back and throw up new stems and foliage each year.

Plants from this region grow well in the garden, often growing much larger than they do in the wild as they lack the intense competition. They do well in ordinary garden soil as long as it is well-drained because although often running with water, the meadows are free-draining with little stagnant water. In the main they are spring flowering and do not mind being overshadowed by other plants later in the season.

Around and above the meadows are the woodlands and forests that clothe the sides of the mountain, rising up to the levels where the trees can no longer live. Here again there is plenty of nutrients washed down with the melting snows and plenty of humus, particularly resulting from decaying leaves. At lower elevations the trees tend to be deciduous, but the most common are the evergreen conifers. Not much grows under the latter except at the margins or in clearings where the light can penetrate, but under the deciduous trees there are many of the woodland flowers. These tend to be spring flowering, doing so before the leaves on the trees unfurl. In the garden these plants are suitble for shady areas or under deciduous shrubs and trees. They like to have a rich leaf-mould soil and make ideal plants for a peat bed. Many alpine gardeners grow woodland plants with great success and much pleasure but it is an area that many people do not associate with alpines until they start growing them.

Emerging from the trees one comes into a sub-alpine level with a scrubby vegetation, often including rhododendrons and dwarf conifers. This merges with the upland pastures, which unlike their lowland counterparts have a sparser, compact herbage, but they are still relatively rich in minerals and many interesting plants grow there. This area merges with the bare rocks of the mountain proper where only occasional pockets of grass occur. Eventually all grassland is left behind and any plants that grow do so in odd pockets of detritus or with deep roots penetrating down through crevices or screes. Here the plants are open to the harsh elements and have a short growing season, hence the plants tend to be small and compact, often putting out their flowers as soon as the snow clears. There is no time for the large herbaceous plant to send up all its growth. There are fewer situations that will support plant life and so there is not much competition; once a plant has established itself it is unlikely to have fierce neighbours. In cultivation these high mountain alpines dislike competition and any threatening gestures from large plants or weeds will make the alpine quickly succumb.

Plants have adapted to different situations often sending down roots a long way into the rock in search of nourishment and to act as an anchor. This latter is particularly important for those plants that grow on moving screes; those jumbles of rocks that are constantly tinkling and creaking as they move, like dry glaciers. On these the top of the plant can be many metres below the tips of their roots as the plants are moved downhill by the slipping scree.

Where the screes are more fixed, such as on more gentle slopes, there will be odd pockets of detritus amongst the jumble of rocks and roots again will delve down to find nourishment and moisture. Similarly in the fissures of rocks, minute roots will penetrate down through the narrowest of cracks to search out the moisture below. Not all the fissures and crevices are minute, sometimes they are quite wide and a cumulation of detritus will enable plants to get a foothold.

In spite of looking very barren and dry, in all these situations there is generally some water throughout most of the year trickling beneath the rocks, even in the winter when the surface, above the snow, is well below freezing. This moisture not only provides water for the plants but also tends to leach away the nutrients down the mountain, to the benefit of the meadow plants but leaving the higher plants with a sparse diet. From this then, we can generally conclude that high alpines should be kept watered but not overfed. Overfeeding will not only result in untypical plants, they may well look like cabbages rather than alpines, but the ensuing lush growth opens up the plant to all kind of predators and diseases.

Of course these conditions are not only found on the upper slopes; there are often areas free of trees lower down the slopes, such as cliff faces which are ideal places for the small alpines to grow. Amongst the meadows there will often be found rocky outcrops and man-made gorges, or passes for traffic supply a suitable habitat for what would normally be some of the higher alpines.

So go to the mountains if you can. It is not essential for your gardening but it will certainly add to your knowledge and ability as well as your pleasure.

2 The Rock Garden

The rock garden is the traditional way of growing alpine plants. It was introduced in Victorian times, not so much as a place to grow alpines but more as a feature in the garden. But it was soon taken over by those who were more interested in growing plants than looking at a heap of rocks. The form was developed during the early part of the present century, but has gone out of favour with many growers who prefer to grow their plants either in pots or on raised beds, which perform the same function but are not so natural-looking or easy to integrate into the garden. Having said that, it is not always easy to merge a rock garden into the overall design, particularly if you live in a flat area. In some countries, in particular Czecho-slovakia, the construction of rock gardens has become a high-art form and nearly all the plants are grown in this way.

There are several points that are considered by some gardeners to count against rock gardens. One is financial; it can cost a lot of money to buy suitable rock particularly if you do not live in an area where stone is quarried; but once purchased you have it for ever, there is no need to renew it. The second objection that is often raised is that they are the devil to weed and maintain. To a certain extent this is true. Once weeds, particularly rhizomous ones, get their toes down beneath the rocks they can be extremely difficult to remove. Most people that dislike rock gardens have at sometime or other acquired a plant or plants that have fallen in love with their new home and romped everywhere, often necessitating the complete disman-tling of the rockwork to eradicate it. The important thing is to stay in control. It is essential to clean the ground and surrounding area of pernicious weeds before you start and constant vigilance, rather than a once a year blitz, should prevent too many problems with weeds. The problem of over-enthusiastic plants is more difficult to solve. I think it behoves every rock gardener to keep a list of such thugs and whenever he hears a whisper that a certain plant is liable to run, it should be added to his proscribed list.

There are equally strong arguments in favour of a rock garden. If well-constructed they can look magnificent and can certainly be an asset in any garden. They can be made to blend in better than a raised bed with the rest of the garden. And, possibly of most importance, they can provide a range of habitats that it is virtually impossible to produce in any other way. The rocks provide warmth, shade, cool root-runs, drainage, and a backdrop from which to show off the plant. If constructed and planted correctly, rockwork should last for many many years without major work needed on it.

With time and patience a rock garden can be created which will not only give a great deal of pleasure but which will provide an ideal habitat for the plants, They have been a little out of favour in recent years, but I think the time is right for a revival and soon they will be seen again in all their glory.

X

Choice of Site

Before doing anything else, the choice of site must be carefully considered. There are so many things to avoid that perhaps you may well throw up your hands in horror and announce that it will not fit into your garden. The main priority is that it should be in as open a position as possible, to catch all the sun and air going. Overhanging trees, shady walls and fences are best avoided, unless you are specialising in shade lovers. Trees, although useful for woodland plants, are anathema to rock gardens. They not only shade the bed, but produce a drip when it rains, which most alpines will not tolerate. Trees are also hungry feeders and their roots will soon get in amongst the rocks, removing any moisture and nutrients. So keep away from trees and large bushes. The plants, unlike the gardener, can stand quite a lot of wind, indeed they must have air circulating around them, but in excessive windy and draughty spots (particularly caused by gaps between buildings) they should be given some sort of protection. A hedge is the best form of windbreak, but it should not be too near the rock garden otherwise its thirsty roots will penetrate the rockwork.

Cold should not be a problem with most alpine plants, but frost hollows should be avoided, not so much because of the frost but because these areas are also likely to be damp with stagnant air. In some cases such pockets of air can be 'drained' by opening a gap in the hedge or fence on the lower side of the hollow.

The other thing to avoid is very wet areas. Although the rock garden will be raised up above the surrounding soil level it is still best not to site it on top of a permanently damp spot, otherwise the water will rise up through the soil and rocks leaving the roots of the plants permanently wet. As long as it is well-drained, it does not matter on what type of soil the rock garden is built.

The best site is on an existing slope where the rock looks like a natural outcrop and blends in with the surroundings, but it is more than possible to construct it on the flat without its looking out of place.

Other factors are more aesthetic and will be considered under the section on design, but it must be said here that the position of the rock garden should enable it to blend in with the rest of the garden. Indeed, the best way to achieve this is to turn the whole of your plot into a rock garden.

Choice of Rock

Making a rock garden blend in with the surroundings is very important if you want to achieve a natural look. One of the major factors in achieving this is the right choice of stone. The first criterion should be that it is a local stone. The main reason for this is that local stone will be more in harmony with its surroundings; it will look at home with the native soil and any outcrops in the area. The second point about local stone is that if it comes from a quarry near you, you have the opportunity of going and selecting the pieces you want; you can choose the size, shape and graining, rather than having random pieces tipped at your gate. The third reason in favour of local stone is that it is bound to be cheaper. Most of the expense when buying stone goes into the transportation costs; the farther it comes the more you will be charged. If you have your own transport that can take several tonnes of rock then you are in the best position of all.

It is always best to choose a natural stone, avoid lumps of concrete and certainly the plastic 'stones' that are now available. I have seen gardens where concrete has been blended in well but it takes a lot of skill. As to plastic, it might look like stone at a hundred metres but it has none of its properties that are essential to the plants' wellbeing.

Avoid using too soft a stone. Anything that is porous can be shattered in the frosts. Nothing is worst than slaving over the construction of a superb rock garden, only to find it reduced to rubble during a cold winter. (It can of course always then be used as a scree bed!) Some of the softer limestones are liable to release a small amount of lime into the soil. This is generally of no problem as many alpines thrive in this type of condition, but it does rule out the possibility of growing ericaceous plants, such as rhododendrons, on the rock garden. There is less of a problem with the harder limestones.

Lucky is he that has a choice of stone. The best stone to use is that which has some apparent stratification such as sandstone or limestone, of which limestone is usually considered the best. Sandstones are usually a warm colour with variations from almost white to dark brown. Limestone also has variation in colour, this time from white to dark greys, but generally it is a colder looking stone. Granite can be considered but is a more unyielding stone and, while it can be used, it is difficult to use sympathetically. The over-riding factors are the stone's ability to fit in with its surroundings, the personal preference on the part of the owner and availability.

If possible go to the quarry and select your own stone. If you just order it, you may find that it is all awkward shapes and sizes. You will certainly find that you are paying for plenty of small pieces and dust that you will not want. When selecting rock, choose the biggest pieces that you can move. The bigger the rocks, the more natural the outcrop will look. Choose those pieces that have at least one good face to present to the world and, if possible, ones that have already been weathered. This last condition is not too important as the stone will soon acquire the patina of age.

Soil

The soil is a very important element in a rock garden and just as much consideration should be given to it as the rock. The type of soil on which the rock garden is constructed is generally of little consequence as long as it is well-drained, and will be considered in the next section. The soil used in the construction is another matter. It should be a friable, well-drained soil and yet moisture retentive. 'Well-drained and moisture retentive' sounds like a contradiction, but is an expression that crops up time and time again in alpine gardening. What it means is that the soil should be able to retain a certain amount of moisture, usually held in the particles of humus, such as peat, at the same time any excess or free water should be able to drain away so that there is no stagnant water around the roots of plants. The degree of drainage needed depends on the plant.

If the existing garden soil is really heavy or excessively chalky, then the easiest solution is to import some good loamy topsoil. Sandy and light soils can be improved by adding leaf-mould and other humus. Clay and chalky soils can be improved by the addition of grit or sharp sand and, once again, humus. The aim should be to get the best possible soil; a good loam. To this should be added more grit to help with the drainage and leaf-mould or peat to help with moisture retention. The mix should be roughly one part of good loam, one part of grit and one part leaf-mould or peat. You will want to vary this mixture in different parts of the rock garden to give different conditions, for example more leaf-mould or peat can be added to certain pockets, particularly those in the shade, where the plants are likely to require more moisture. Similarly more grit can be added in other places to create more arid conditions that certain plants require.

We will come on to a detailed discussion of feeding in a later section, but it must also be considered briefly at this stage, because once constructed the rock garden will remain in place for many years, and the soil will not be renewed. Many alpine gardeners are against any form of fertilisers and rely entirely on the existing nutrients in the soil and the breakdown of the leaf-mould. Others would add small quantities of a slow-release fertiliser to the soil at this stage. If you are intending to grow just the high alpines then it is probably best not to use any feed, but if you are going to plant many of the more lowland and woodland plants then some addition would be of benefit. Again the composition can be varied so that some pockets are richer than others.

The main thing to remember is that the soil must be prepared carefully for the rock garden. It is no use constructing it with a heap of soil left over from the digging of a pool or house foundations (unless, of course, you are lucky enough to have loam down to these depths). If you have any doubts about your own soil, import some of better quality and then add grit and humus.

Design

The design of the rock garden is entirely a personal matter. Some of the original rock gardens were designed to look like miniature mountain ranges, in some cases faithful reproductions of the Matterhorn and other favourite mountains were created. To the modern eye this smacks of the equivalent of using garden gnomes as part of the design.

The overall effect should be as natural-looking as possible within the confines of a garden setting. If it can look like an outcrop of the local rock emerging from the ground, so much the better. The basic ideal is to place the rock all sloping at the same angle and with the strata all running in the same direction.

The rocks should tilt back into the slope; this sends the water back into the outcrop, rather than shedding over the face which will not only be a waste of water but in all probability cause erosion of the soil on the terraces and crevices below. The rocks can be laid close on top of one another to form, more or less, a steep bluff with just a few planting pockets or the layers can be spread out with small plateaux

The rock should tilt back into the bed, forming a steep bluff one side and a gentle slope on the other

Rock garden built into an existing bank

in between giving larger planting areas. The latter is of course cheaper as the rock goes farther. An excellent compromise can be reached where these are combined giving a greater variety of planting places.

Undoubtedly the use of existing banks makes the best-looking gardens, but it is possible to make the outcrop emerge out of a flat piece of ground, with a steep face towards the south and a gentler slope tailing away to the north. In free-draining areas it is also possible to excavate out a ravine and build the rockwork up on either side of the path. This can be very effective if you have the space and energy. As a

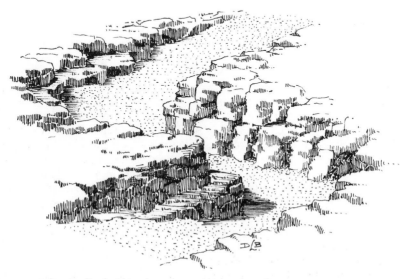

An excavated ravine lined with rocks makes an ideal rock garden

17

A limestone pavement is a level rock garden with planting pockets

contrast one can construct the equivalent of a limestone pavement which is built flat on the site. This can provide some interesting niches for the plants but does not look so effective as the other two methods.

Blending in with the rest of the garden is very difficult. It is often suggested that the immediate area around the rock garden is left as rough grass but I have always been against this because of the perpetual threat of the grass moving in on to the rockwork. It is possible to compromise and have an intermediate scree area of rough stones. Certainly the outcrop will be incongruous if it is surrounded by herbaceous borders, but it is possible gradually to scale it up to larger plants particularly using dwarf shrubs as a transitional planting.

It is helpful to get some rough impression of what you are going to do on paper before you start, even the most amateurish of sketches can help you get some idea of where the main rocks are going to be (remember you want to move the rock as little as possible — if only for the sake of your back).

Construction

There are three aspects of construction to be considered: the site preparation, the physical movement of the stone and, finally, the layout and form of the rock garden itself.

Two things are essential in the preparation of any site: first the total removal of any perennial weeds and second the provision of adequate drainage.

Once the rock garden has been constructed it is very difficult to remove any persistent weeds without taking it apart. It is possible to use weedkillers but this is very risky with alpine plants about, so be certain to prepare carefully before construction begins. At this stage it is possible to use chemical herbicides as there are no plants (other than weeds) involved. If you dislike using them then a large sheet of black polythene spread over the site for several months will have the same effect. It is possible to dig and remove everything by hand if the soil is friable enough, but it is very easy to leave fragments of the roots in the soil which will mature at about the same time as you finish the rockwork.

Drainage is important but it can be over-stressed. The rock garden is being built on top of the existing soil level so unless the garden is very wet it should not be affected. If your garden is wet with either running or stagnant water then you ought to consider draining the whole thing properly otherwise, apart from bog gardening,

18

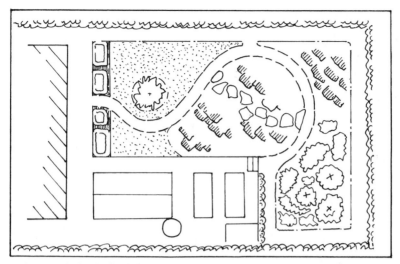

Make a rough sketch plan before you start construction

you are going to be very limited in what you can do. If it is just the area where you intend to put the rock garden that is wet then you can give this local drainage. There is little point in just digging a hole under the site and filling it with rubble as it inevitably will act as a sump and fill up with water. Such a hole should be dug and then it should be provided with a pipe or a rubble-filled channel to take the water away downhill, either to be released into the open ground or into a soakaway (a large hole filled with rubble). In the majority of gardens this will probably be unnecessary, but if in doubt add drainage.

Moving stone is a very heavy and dangerous task and should not be undertaken without realising that without care back and other injuries can be sustained. Heavier stone should not be lifted; it is quite possible to manoeuvre it into any position by rolling it or by using levers. Even putting large lumps on the top of the construction can be achieved by building temporary ramps of earth. If you really want to use very heavy pieces of stone then hire some mechanical device such as a JCB to help you.

One of the simplest devices for moving stone is the lever; a stout pole with a fulcrum (another piece of rock) placed under it about a third of the way up its length. Rocks can be moved quite a distance using this method or just a centimetre

Moving heavy lumps of stone with a lever or on rollers

19

for final positioning. Large rocks can be levered on to rollers, short metal scaffold poles or round wooden poles, and pushed. Smaller rocks can be rolled, which involves only lifting a part of the weight. It is as well to have more than one person to help when heavy stone is being moved. Watch for your fingers when you are moving one piece of stone up against another; trapping them is surprisingly easy and can be a very painful business.

If possible it helps to spread the rock out around you before you start constructing so that you can see what you have got. If it is left in a heap you will be forever moving it in your search for the right piece. This is a tremendous waste of effort and can be very tiring.

Build the first layer packing the soil down between the rocks, if possible leaving no crevices or holes for slugs to live. The stones should be well bedded in with a slope back into the structure. If there are visible strata lines in the rock then these should be horizontal. At least a third of each piece should be buried by the soil. Before moving on ensure that the rocks are steady and do not rock; they should be able to take your weight without moving. This generally means that when placing the rocks, the widest side is used as the base, but sometimes aesthetics dictate otherwise and this is all right as long as the stone is stable.

The second layer is added sticking to the overall plan that you have devised. There will be some variation to this plan as the shape of the individual pieces of stone will have a strong influencing factor on the finished appearance. Keep the stones as close together as possible. Remember to vary the mixture of your infill material if you want to create different types of habitat.

To the grower of alpines, the rock is more than a visual memory of the plants' original home. Plants like the cool root-run it provides and the moisture it retains beneath the surface. There is a natural tendency to use expensive rock only on the surface of the outcrop where it can be seen, but it is also useful to have rock actually inside the structure partly to give the searching roots the rocks they seek but also to support the heavy stones on the top of the structure. If there is only soil beneath them they will tip or even sink and what started as a rocky outcrop will end up looking like a limestone pavement! The point is that below the surface any stone or rock can be used, even lumps of concrete, leaving the dearly purchased rock for the surface layers.

It may be necessary to build a temporary ramp of earth over part of the lower layers if you want to roll larger stones to the top of the construction. Take your time over this work, partly because it can be tiring but also because it is essential to stand back every so often and have a look at what you have done; it is easier to correct a mistake as you go than when the rockwork is finished.

When all the rock and soil is in position you are ready to topdress with gravel or chippings. If you are going to plant straightaway it is best to wait until the construction is finished then cover all the exposed soil with 2.5cm (1in) or so of chippings. The type and colour should match the rockwork; avoid using limestone chippings on a sandstone rock garden. If you are not planting immediately then topdress and scrape back this cover when you plant, replacing it when the job is complete. This topdressing acts as a mulch preserving moisture and keeping weeds down, serves as a dry collar around the plant, helping to prevent it from rotting, and provides an attractive background against which the plant is displayed.

Planting

The whole purpose of a rock garden is to provide a natural habitat for certain types of plants, namely alpines and other low-growing species. What you can grow will be considered in a moment, but first we must look at the process of getting the plants into the ground.

There are two approaches: planting as the rock garden is being constructed or waiting until all the construction work is finished and then setting about furnishing it. The advantage of planting as you go is that it allows you to 'build' plants into the right crevices and cracks which is a very difficult operation when the rocks are in position. The disadvantages are that you are bound to tread on some plants as work proceeds and you will possibly change your mind as to where you want a plant after you have finished, when it will be impossible to extricate. Another problem is that if at any stage you are not satisfied with the rockwork you are likely to dismantle it, disturbing the plant which will be losing soil from its roots and drying out all the while.

I personally favour building up the complete structure then looking at it as a whole and deciding on the best layout for the plants. You can stand the plants in their pots all over the bed which makes it easier to visualise the finished effect and shuffle things around, with no damage, while you decide on the best position for each. Having said that, I think there is a strong case for inserting a few of the crevice-lovers as you go if you are certain where you want them. The plants should have been well watered some time before they are needed. After extraction from their pots some of the soil can be removed or the rootball gently compressed into a narrow oval shape. This can then be inserted between rocks as they are brought together. Add extra compost around the rootball, ensuring that the roots have contact with soil within the bed thus enabling them to grow away into the mass of the rock garden. Water as soon as convenient.

Vary the amount of drainage material and humus in the various pockets of soil so that different types of plant can be placed in different positions. For example, shade lovers that require more moisture can be planted on the shady side of a rock or at the north side of the rock garden with a little extra leaf-mould or peat added to the soil. Similarly those that revel in hot dry conditions should be planted on the southern faces where they will get maximum sunshine, and extra grit can be added for the true arid dwellers.

Avoid planting in the heat of the day and make certain that the plants do not dry out, particularly in the first few days when the rock may well be taking up any of the free moisture in the soil.

It is important to label the plants as they are put in. It is surprising how quickly one can forget the particulars of a plant. (Details on labelling are given on p. 87).

Maintenance

Once the rock garden has been built and planted, there is, unfortunately, more to do than simply sitting back and enjoying it. Fortunately, if it was constructed with care and a little attention is given regularly, the task will not be too onerous. Mind you, I always enjoy tinkering around pulling out the odd weed or doing a bit of pruning. If you are close enough to do these things you will see a lot more and appreciate your plants more than if you admire them from a distance. Getting your hands dirty is undoubtedly the best way of enjoying both your garden and your gardening.

Watering

I was amazed to see a well-known 'media' gardener stating in print recently that the advantage of alpines was that they never needed watering, even in dry weather. The number of plants he must have killed does not bear thinking about, but then with advice like that it seems unlikely that he has ever grown any.

Alpines need water. And they need it regularly. The reason for this is that we have deliberately made the soil free-draining to protect the plant from stagnant water and the small amount of water held in the humus can be used up very quickly, particularly in hot weather. The bed should have about 2.5cm (1in) of water every ten days or so, more in really hot and drying weather. Overhead sprays are the most efficient way of giving it; a watering can is laborious for a large area and certain parts may only receive a superficial sprinkling. Make certain the bed receives a good dousing; five minutes is worse than useless. If you live in a very dry area then it might be worth while installing a permanent sprinkler system; unsightly, but functional.

Feeding

This is a very controversial subject amongst alpine gardeners, but while many might deny feed to their pot plants which have a change of compost every year, few would forgo feeding their rock gardens or raised beds where the plants stay in the same soil for many years. The nutrients are not only used up by the plants but are leached away by the rain and these should be replenished to keep the plants healthy.

It is advisable not to use too strong a nitrogenous fertiliser as the plants will grow too lush. Because great quantities are not needed it is best to use a slow-release fertiliser, such as bonemeal, or a general fertiliser with an equal balance of nitrogen, phosphorus and potassium.

Whatever is used it should be only used sparingly. The best time for application is in the late winter before the plants have started into growth. It should be scattered by hand, being careful not to get any on the plants themselves. It is best carried out in conjunction with renewal of the topdressing.

Mulching

The conventional gardener's approach to mulching is to apply a good layer of farmyard manure, but covering your rock garden with muck would do it no good at all! In our context, mulching is with gravel or stone chips.

Mulching has several points in its favour: (1) it prevents the soil from panning in heavy rain or watering; (2) it preserves moisture; (3) it prevents water lying around the collars of plants, i.e. it helps prevent plants rotting around the neck; (4) it suppresses weeds and when they do grow it is easier to get them out; (5) it provides a good background against which to display the plants.

Normally one would use a material which is sympathetic in colour with the main rockwork, i.e. gravel for sandstone and limestone chippings for limestone. It would normally be applied when the rock garden is constructed, but it is slowly drawn down into the bed by the action of worms and the weather and so needs replacing or at least replenishing each year. Do not use limestone chippings if you are growing ericaceous plants.

The late winter is the best time to apply it and I normally go over the surface removing any weeds or unwanted seedlings, adding a little fertiliser and finally topping up the dressing.

The humus in the soil gets broken down and disappears leaving a mixture of loam and grit, so it is advantageous to add a small dressing of this every other year before applying the grit mulch. It can be worked into the top of the soil, but where there is a chance of damaging roots it is best left to the worms who will do the job for you.

Weeding

Little and often is the answer. With good preparation, mulching with grit and regular inspections there should be little problem. Where problems do occur is when the bed is left to its own devices for a year or more and spreading weeds get into the soil and between the rocks; it then becomes virtually impossible to manage, all you can do is a cosmetic job by removing the tops of the weeds, and after about four days you have to do it all again. If you get to that situation you will have to grit your teeth and decide either to give up rock gardening altogether or to break it down and start again.

There are one or two simple measures you can take besides the all-important precaution of starting off with weed-free soil. When you are given or buy plants, always check that there is no weed root lurking in the rootball. It is very easy, for example, to have a small piece of couch grass or ground elder in a plant that someone has kindly dug up for you. This will uncontrollably infest the whole garden if you do not spot it. Similarly be certain that no creeping weeds can move in from outside your garden, or, indeed, from other parts of your garden. Weed seed will be blown in and carried in, unseen, on other plants but the resulting seedlings are easily spotted and can be dealt with before they become anything like a nuisance.

Avoid using weedkillers anywhere near alpine plants. However careful you are, there will always be some that goes in the wrong place and the slightest drift can cause untold damage.

Winter protection

Alpine plants are generally hardy and should not want any winter protection from straightforward coldness. Wind is one of the worst enemies of plants, and there should be protection from strong, cold winds. Another problem is that there is no way of preventing plants coming into growth early due to a warm spell, then having their new growth cut back by a sudden reversal to cold weather. Valuable plants that do this may need covering during any subsequent frosts.

If you are in doubt as to a plant's hardiness keep it in an alpine house or a cold frame until you have propagated up sufficient numbers to try some outside. Some growers group any plants they suspect of possibly being a bit tender in one or two places in the rock garden, and cover them with a polythene frame on nights when they suspect the temperature is going to go too far below freezing. This protection is usually sufficient to see most things through the winter.

Where protection is needed is for those plants that are prone to die if they get too damp. The best way of coping with this problem is to cover them with a sloping sheet of glass, anchored down against the wind. The sides should be open to allow the free passage of air.

The philosophy of many gardeners, for which I have quite a lot of sympathy, is only to grow hardy plants. If a plant dies through cold they will try it again, just in

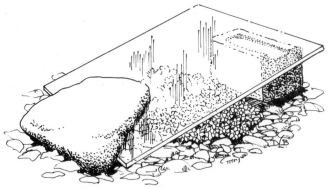

A sheet of glass will protect individual plants from excessive wet

case that was a particularly weak plant or there was some other reason for its death. Perhaps they might try it in a warmer spot. If it succumbs again, they will not bother to give it another chance.

It is worth remembering that not all plants of the same species will have the same tolerance to cold. For example plants grown from seed collected from near the top of a mountain will probably be hardier than those from seed collected lower down. So do not give up hope if something that you particularly want to grow dies on you. Try a plant from a different source or get seed from plants that are known to be hardy.

Hardiness is a complex business and one should not despair too much over losses. Apart from anything else if a plant dies it does mean that you have a space for another!

Soil renewal

If properly constructed and maintained the rock garden should last many years without renewal, but it may be necessary from time to time to rake out the old soil from some pockets where vigorous plants have exhausted or soured it and replace it with a fresh mixture. It is also possible to take to pieces part of the rock garden each year and thus renew the whole thing over a period of years.

Plants

What plants can or should be grown on a rock garden? This is entirely up to you. If you are starting out then I would suggest that you concentrate on the easier-to-grow plants and gain experience with growing these before tackling the more difficult species. There is as much pleasure to be had from these easier plants; rarer plants are not necessarily more beautiful, often they are not, but they are more difficult to grow and even experienced growers lose plants which are not only expensive but often difficult to replace.

The plants listed at the end of the book are nearly all suitable for the rock garden; if not it is mentioned in the text. Choose what you want and ensure they get the situation they require: sun, shade, a vertical crevice, and so on. I do not want to give you a list at this stage, because the garden you are constructing is yours and not mine, and selecting the right plants is all part of the learning process. You will make some mistakes and put plants in the wrong place either for their needs or for their appearance but that is how it should be. You must not worry as you will learn more from making mistakes than from accidentally getting it right first time.

Sooner or later, as well as maintaining your general collection, you are going to want to specialise in one genus or another; in other words to try and collect all the species, hybrids and cultivars of one genus. This can be a very valuable way of learning about plants because you will become aware of the often minute variations that differentiate one species from the other; you will begin to look at the plants more closely. Again do not be tempted to run before you can walk and go for the complex, difficult genera like dionysias or androsaces. Choose something simple and preferably something that is not too promiscuous so that you do not have masses of hybrids to confuse you and make identification very difficult. Try not to go too mad and fill the whole rock garden with the same genus to the exclusion of other plants!

3 The Alpine House

It is not essential to have an alpine house to grow alpine plants; many of the best growers do without them, but houses do have two or three advantages. They protect the gardener from the worst excesses of the weather, they offer protection to the plants and, by the use of staging, they bring the plants up to a height where they can be more easily appreciated by the eye and the nose as well as being more easily cared for.

The idea of protection for the gardener may seem fanciful, but much of the time spent tending and appreciating alpine plants is during the late winter and early spring when the weather can be decidedly unpleasant. The fact that the grower can be under cover is usually very much appreciated, particularly on a sunny day when there is a strong, cold wind blowing.

Some plants also need a certain amount of protection. This need not necessarily be against the cold but against the damp, which kills as many plants as frost. In many cases it is not a matter of life or death but more a matter of looking one's best. Plants which flower early, such as *Ranunculus calindrioides,* often have delicate petals which can be ruined if left in the open garden. With the protection of glass they can be in peak condition. This is particularly important, of course, if you are thinking of showing plants. Surprisingly some plants, particularly bulbs, need protection in the summer — from the rain. These will be looked at in more detail under the section on bulb frames.

Most plants are grown in pots on raised benches and this provides a good height for looking at and smelling the plants. Such an arrangement is not entirely for aesthetic considerations, some plants need constant attention and problems such as pests can be more readily seen if closer at hand. One of the keys to success in growing alpines is keen observation and it is undoubtedly easier to do this in an alpine house where one can be in very close contact with the subject.

Growing plants in alpine houses is usually undertaken in one of two ways: in pots or in beds. Undoubtedly the commonest method is the use of pots but many growers have succeeded in making miniature rock gardens within the alpine house. These can either be built on the floor on either side of the central gangway or raised on staging. These can look very attractive but they do need a lot of attention, particularly to watering and pests and diseases. Both these methods will be considered in detail later in the chapter.

Structure of the Alpine House

What is an alpine house and how does one set about acquiring or making one? Buying an alpine house is undoubtedly a major undertaking these days. A custom-made one is very expensive indeed. It is much cheaper to buy a conventional greenhouse and modify it.

The basic purpose of the house is to provide shelter from the elements (wind, rain, frost and sun), at the same time letting in as much light and air as possible. Since the idea is not to provide an airtight box a simple glass roof, like a bus shelter, will suffice as long as the site is not too windy. However, it is normal to use a conventional structure with glass walls and roof.

I am certain that the old maxim about buying greenhouses still holds true today. 'Think of the size you want, then double it.' It is possible to grow alpines in a very small house, but the problem is that one's interests, and collection, is always growing and a second house is soon required. The only advice one can give is to buy the largest you can afford (bearing in mind the cost of any modifications you may need to make) and the space and position in the garden allows. It is worth remembering that it is possible to work with the combination of cold frames and alpine house, where plants are generally kept in frames and only brought into the house while in flower or when in need of attention.

Siting the alpine house is important and will involve many personal consider-ations, particularly that of the layout and design of the garden. Greenhouses are usually shoved at the bottom of the garden tucked away behind some form of screen. Fine if you do not want to see it and only occasionally venture into it, but if you are going to become an active grower you will be visiting it possibly every day, often in the winter or of an evening after work, so it is more convenient to have it near the house. In the winter it will obviously be dark in the evening so closeness to the house will facilitate the supply of electricity for lighting.

It should be in an open position where it can get as much light as possible. The difficulty with this is that the more light you achieve, the more sunshine you will get and hence heat. To avoid this one has to have recourse to some form of shading. Some people advocate placing the house near a deciduous tree that will cast a natural light shade over the glass. This is fine in a sunny district but in a summer that is overcast there is no way of removing the leaves to allow enough light to reach the benches. The orientation of an alpine house is not too critical although the usual greenhouse axis of east-west is generally preferred: to allow maximum sunshine to enter in the winter.

Hopefully you intend to use your alpine house for many years so it makes sense to put it on a firm base. Certainly the sides should have a solid foundation and it is recommended that the whole of the base is concreted over. There are several reasons for this. The main one is that the weight of the benching with its wet plunge material and the full pots is considerable and will need foundations to prevent its piers sinking into the ground. Another reason is that it makes it easier to keep the floor both clean and tidy; an important consideration in the fight against pests and diseases.

While making the base it is worth giving some thought to a path from the house to the alpine house; it can be very muddy walking to and fro. Similarly it is useful to have a solid area near to the alpine house on which things can be put down or compost mixed.

The materials from which the supporting framework is made are of little consequence; some people prefer wood because it looks more natural, others prefer aluminium because it is easy to maintain. I do not think it makes any difference to the plants one way or the other. If you are going to grow some plants that will need some heat (most alpine growers would shudder at the thought) or live in an area where the temperatures can be really cruel, then a wooden house will be marginally warmer.

Many of the older alpine houses were partially excavated from the ground. In practice it was only the centre gangway that was dug out and you entered by going down some steps. This had two effects. The first was that there was less vertical walling, hence it was cheaper and there was less heat loss. The second was that the staging was actually at ground level which meant that the plunge material was resting on the solid earth. This does away with the need for strong supports and keeps the plunge much warmer in the winter as it is no longer surrounded top and bottom with cold air; the ground also acts as a storage heater. Because such greenhouses are not made for the mass market they are very expensive today, although you could make one yourself. Another problem is that you must have a well-drained site, otherwise you might have to swim between the benches.

Ventilation

Ventilation is one of the most crucial considerations when buying or making an alpine house. It is important on two counts: first it does not allow damp, stagnant air to accumulate and, secondly, it prevents the house from getting too hot on summer days. The conventional greenhouse seems to be supplied with one door and one or possibly two opening lights in the roof. This is woefully inadequate. There should be doors, or at least a door and an opening window, at both ends to allow a good circulation of air through the house. Ideally there should be a set of opening lights along both sides of the ridge and another set on both of the side walls at bench height. If this can be achieved then you will have a superb alpine house.

As I have already said, custom-built alpine houses are expensive and so if you buy a conventional greenhouse then all this extra ventilation will have to be added. In many cases you can buy louvred units to replace individual panes of glass on the side panels and ordinary opening lights to go on the roof. Even if you can only afford to do every other one, this is better than nothing. If you are sheltered from driving rain, then there is the simple expedient of removing one or more panes of glass for the summer and replacing it during the winter. Certainly this is one way of coping with the end opposite the door. If you do take out glass remember to cover the opening with wire-netting to prevent birds and animals getting in.

The time that greatest ventilation is required is in the summer, but it is also needed during the winter. Depending on what you grow it should not be necessary to shut the house up completely unless it gets very cold. I never close the doors unless there is the likelihood of snow drifting in, as I do not grow anything that will not take quite a degree of frost. Driving rain can also be a nuisance but it is usually possible to keep open all the ventilation on the opposite side to the wind.

If you live in an area where it is sometimes necessary to shut all the ventilation, for example if you suffer from thick, damp fogs, or excessive cold, then it is desirable to have electric fans that will keep the air circulating. It is possible to have these connected to a humidity control which will switch them on automatically when the amount of moisture in the air rises to a danger point for the plants.

Having mentioned the need for the free passage of air, do not take it to extremes and allow a perpetual howling gale to pass through the house — plants dislike a draught as much as humans do.

Light and shade

It would make life easier if we could grow plants in the dark but unfortunately they all need light. The amount varies: woodlanders will take a degree of shade but many of the high alpine plants get a great deal of light, uninterrupted by the thin and unpolluted mountain air. So for alpines our house should let in the maximum amount of light and preferably from all directions. If the main source comes from one side then plants will grow towards that source and become drawn and leggy. This is why it is best to locate the alpine house in an open position, and why lean-to houses are not always satisfactory. Lighting in the latter can be improved by painting the solid wall white.

During the dullest months of the year, namely the winter, the glass should be kept as clean as possible to let in maximum light. One should also strive towards this during the summer but there is another factor that comes into play: the sun. This has two bad effects: its fierce rays can shrivel up the plants and it can make the alpine house unbearably hot.

The effects of the sun can be reduced by introducing some form of screening. There are several methods that can be used, varying in their permanency. The basic idea is that you put up a barrier between the sun and the plant which will cut out the harmful effects of the sun while letting in maximum light. It is nearly always best to do this on the outside of the alpine house. If placed on the inside of the glass the ill-effects from the direct rays will be curbed, but once the sun's rays are through the glass the temperature will rise so you have only cured half the problem.

The easiest and cheapest shading is provided by spraying or painting on a white liquid which, when dry, makes the glass opaque. This works well in sunny weather, allowing ample light in, but in dull weather it reduces the amount of light in the alpine house considerably. If a dull period is expected to last several days then the wash should be removed and reapplied when the weather brightens again. There is now one of these washes that becomes transparent when it is wet, so that more light enters on rainy days, but this does not help with dry overcast weather.

The next type of shading is some form of blinds. These can either be simply pinned over the glass or attached to a roller on the ridge of the house so that they can easily be rolled in or out depending on the weather. Obviously the latter are much more expensive. The former can be some type of netting, which is light enough to be removed if the weather becomes overcast. The net can be pinned or attached directly to the structure of the house, or special frames can be made up which are hooked on to the roof. Green plastic netting is the most commonly available, but white would be better if you can get it (white will reflect the sunlight, green will absorb it). There are different grades, too, which allow differing amounts of light to pass through. Other blinds can be made from grasses, reeds or bamboo. These are heavier and more suitable for being attached to a roller. In both these cases some of the sun is stopped by the blind, while some is allowed to pass through. Since the sun is constantly moving, these rays move across the house and do not concentrate on one place. It is the equivalent to dappled shade from a tree.

The last method is to have frames made up to which are attached wooden lathes. These are easily placed on the roof in sunny weather and act in the same way as blinds by producing a dappled shade.

Shading is important and is worth giving some thought, using the most convenient for you. If you are out at work all day, then you have no opportunity of putting the shades on or taking them off if the weather changes, so you may feel that a spray is all that is needed. On the other hand if you or somebody else can put them on and off, then it might be better to consider one of the more expensive alternatives which will give better results.

Protection from animals

Having managed to keep the weather out some consideration must be given to preventing ingress of animals and birds. This is quite important as, for example, a blackbird can pull a cushion plant apart in a matter of seconds while looking for supposed grubs and insects. Similarly in wet weather, cats will find the plunge a fine alternative to your neighbour's border when looking for a litter tray.

These are all easily kept at bay by covering all openings with netting. It is preferable to use wire-netting or mesh as this will be stronger against determined attacks and will last much longer. The windows can have it permanently placed over them on the inside, but obviously this cannot be done with the doorways. Here it is possible to make up a frame on which wire-netting is stretched and then this is placed over the open doorway. Since it will have to be removed every time one goes in or out, it can be hinged on the side opposite to the door so that you can always have one or the other shut.

Staging

We turn now to the inside of the alpine house. It is perfectly possible to stand the pots of plants on the floor, but this is not only an inconvenient height from the grower's point of view but it means that the plants themselves are a long way from the glass and they will become drawn and out of character. It is much better to have staging at say 75cm (2½ft) from the ground. This can be made of any material that is convenient but it must be strong, particularly if you intend to plunge the pots in sand. The combined weight of 15 or 20cm (6–8in) of wet sand plus the pots is considerable and any flimsy structure will soon collapse.

Staging can be purchased made from steel or aluminium which will adequately take the strain. Alternatively it can be made from wood, in which case the uprights must be thick and treated with wood preservative, but avoid creosote which gives off toxic fumes. The strongest uprights are brick piers. The base of the staging can be made from aluminium sheets, corrugated iron or plastic sheets. At one stage asbestos sheeting was also used but this is frowned upon nowadays for health reasons. Mine consists of a wooden framework lined with aluminium printing plates.

There are two ways of using the staging: either as a plunge bed or simply as a standing place for pots. The plunge bed consists of a depth of 15–20cm (6–8in) of a water retentive material in which the pots are buried almost up to their rims. This has two functions: it allows the pots to absorb moisture from the surrounding plunge and it gives the pots a degree of temperature stability; prevents freezing in winter and keeps them cool in summer.

The commonest used material for this is sharp sand. To this is often added a quantity of either peat or Perlite. Both these will hold moisture better than sand and will keep the plunge moist. This moisture not only helps the plants but also is useful when a pot is removed as it prevents the hole caving in, making it easy to replace the pot in the same place. Another material more commonly used in the past was ash. This will also hold both moisture and its shape.

The other type of staging is where the pots are stood on top of a shallow layer of grit, sharp sand or a capillary mat. Here watering is mainly achieved by applying it to each individual pot. There is no protection against falling or rising temperatures.

Solid wooden staging

It is most useful in areas where deep frosts are unlikely to penetrate the alpine house or for plants that are just 'passing through'. It is also much lighter if you doubt the strength of your staging.

Later in this chapter we will consider the whole question of raised beds within the alpine house, but for the moment I will just record that staging, constructed with deep sides as for plunge material, can be filled with a growing medium, rather than sand, and the plants grown directly in it.

What should one do with the space below the staging? There are several uses for this. If you grow bulbs or other plants that lie dormant for a portion of the year, then these can be stored here, releasing space on the benches. If the walls have glazing right to ground level then there could well be sufficient light for cutting frames to be constructed beneath the benches. It will help with light if the frames can be constructed by digging a pit so that their lids are level with the floor of the house. Heating cables could be included but all this will be discussed later. Some people like to keep their seed pans beneath the benches where they can keep an eye on them.

If you have walls that are solid from bench level downwards then it will be too dark to use it for anything other than storage of dormant plants.

An automatic watering system, using capillary matting and a piece of gutter

Watering systems

Watering itself will be discussed later but here we will just look at the equipment. The majority of people are happy with a simple watering can. Water is obtained from a butt which has collected water from the roof of the alpine house via guttering. In dry weather this will need supplementing from the domestic supply. It is easy and accurate; only the plants that need water get it, but it needs to be done regularly.

If you are out for most of the day or regularly away from home then some automatic system may be required. The simplest is the use of a plunge which is kept moist and which in turn keeps the pots moist. This will hold quite a reserve of water and will not need topping up each day except in very hot weather. Capillary matting can be used, with one edge in a piece of guttering which is kept full of water. The pots stand on the matting and absorb the moisture through the base. With a bit of ingenuity an automatic supply of water from a plastic drum can be made to keep the sand plunge wet or the matting's reservoir full of water.

Another automatic system is to use a mist spray which is connected to the mains and automatically comes on when a special metal strip dries out. This can only be used with plants that do not mind overhead watering.

If all the plants in a particular bed need watering to the same degree, it is possible to flood the bed with 5cm (2in) of water. To achieve this a special watertight bed needs to be constructed. After the pots have drawn up sufficient moisture the excess water is removed by taking out a drainage plug in the base of the bed.

Winter protection

The majority of plants in an alpine house need no further protection, particularly if they are plunged. If the plunge material is resting directly on the earth, such as would be the case in a sunken house, then the protection is all the greater.

However, there are some areas where the winters are severe and others where the odd night can get down to well below freezing. This can do a great deal of damage as the compost in the pots becomes frozen. If they remain frozen for long there is not only the physical stress on the plant but the roots will be unable to take up moisture and the plant will die. The simplest way is to shut down the house before nightfall and to cover the benches with some form of insulation such as bubble polythene or sheets of newspaper. In areas where cold is regularly expected the house should be double glazed with bubble plastic, making certain that the house can still be ventilated during the day.

Individual plants can be given overnight protection by covering them with bottom sections of clear plastic bottles or large glass or plastic jars. If you use two different sizes you get a very good 'double glazing' effect.

If their area is cold enough to require it, many alpine gardeners would allow themselves the assurance of using some form of heating. This would be set so that the thermostat comes on only if the temperature dropped below freezing. In other words the house would not be heated, just frost protected. This protection would be no more than a covering of snow would give in the wild. The simplest way of accomplishing this is to use an electric heater, which with a thermostat set low, is cheap to run, probably cheaper than replacing the plants you might otherwise lose.

Another way of coping with the problem in areas where cold is experienced every year is to put heating cables under the plunge. This will keep the pots from freezing. If a thermostat is added then once it is installed and switched on, it can be left to its own devices and no more attention will be required.

Heat can be used as frost protection, but it is frowned upon to use it to bring on plants for shows.

Maintenance of the house

It goes without saying that the fabric of the house should be kept in good condition. An aluminium house needs little attention apart from replacing any glass that may break. More care is needed for a wooden house. It should be regularly treated with Cuprinol or other wood preservative. This will prevent decay and keep the timbers looking clean and neat. Do *not* use creosote as the fumes are likely to kill off some, if not all, of your plants.

The glass should be kept clean so that the maximum amount of light penetrates down to the bench level. Any wash applied during the summer to keep the sun out should be completely removed during the autumn.

Gutters should be kept cleaned out so that the water in the butt is not contaminated.

On the inside of the house regularly check that the staging is in good condition. If corrugated iron has been used as the base of a plunge, it can corrode and give way. Similarly wooden supports and framework can rot. A jumbled heap of sand, compost, pots and plants is not a welcome sight if the whole lot collapses.

If the plunge is kept moist it is likely that it will become green with algae and moss. This can either be physically removed and replaced with fresh plunge material or sprayed, after removing the pots, with Algofen (UK), which will kill it off.

General hygiene is important. Rubbish, particularly dead leaves and flowers, should not be allowed to litter the floor or accumulate in corners. Such accumulations are a breeding ground for pests and diseases and the simple precaution of making certain that there is none left lying around can pre-empt a lot of trouble.

Propagation frames

Many growers like to have a propagating frame within the alpine house. This can be situated outside but if inside the house there are certain advantages. In the first place it is under cover so the frame has added protection — it is in effect double glazed, which helps to keep the frame warm overnight. Secondly, it is possible to have a power supply in the house which enables the use of heating cables in the frame to help with the rooting of cuttings. Thirdly, if it is built on to the staging, it is at a very convenient height for dealing with fiddly cuttings which are not so easy to manage bending over a frame on the ground.

At its simplest, a cutting frame consists of a wooden box, painted white on the

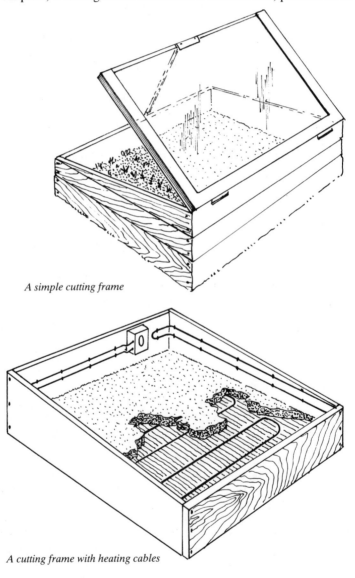

A simple cutting frame

A cutting frame with heating cables

inside to maximise the light, with a hinged lid into which is set a pane of glass. The lid is often sloping to allow any condensation to run to the edge of the frame rather than dripping on to the cuttings. The lid should be provided with a hook or a prop to keep it open while work is being done within the frame. The base of the frame is filled with a cutting compost, usually a 50 : 50 mixture of sharp sand and peat, to a depth of 7.5cm (3in).

A more sophisticated frame can be made along the same lines but by adding electric heating cables in the bottom of the frame, below the planting level, and another set around the inside of the frame above the sand/peat level. They are both connected to thermostats which keeps the sand and the air above them at even temperatures. This shortens the time needed for cuttings to form roots. If the whole frame is not taken up with cuttings during the winter it can be used to plunge one or two of the more tender plants which will appreciate the extra protection of the heating cables and the extra sheet of glass between them and the colder air.

Cuttings should be provided with maximum light but away from direct sunlight. It might be necessary to give the frame its own shading if the main house is sometimes left unshaded.

The most convenient position for cutting frames is on the staging but space may be at a premium, so it is possible to place them below the bench as long as there is adequate light. If they are sunk into the ground so that the lid is at floor level, then the frame will get maximum light from the glazed walls of the house, particularly if it is in the corner where it will get light from two walls and the central gangway. Plants raised in such an under-bench frame should not be left there too long after rooting as they can get drawn.

Growing in Pots

Most alpine gardeners grow some plants in pots, even if they are young plants that they are growing-on ready for planting out in the rock garden. The big advantage is that you can give a plant much more individual attention. You can pick it up, examine it, give it a specific amount when watering, and so on. Unlike a plant permanently in the ground, it is possible regularly to turn a pot round so that the plant gets an even supply of light, thus creating a more symmetrically-shaped plant, if that is your wish (for showing purposes perhaps).

Pots are also mobile so it is possible to take the plants to shows or to bring them indoors for use briefly as table or other decorations. The latter use is particularly appreciated in the winter and early spring, but plants should not be left inside the house too long otherwise the dry air from the central heating will soon desiccate the plant. Some plants seem to do better in the limited space of a pot. Perhaps this is because they are used to restricted root space in their native habitat; growing in crevices for example.

Types of pots

Amongst any gathering of alpine growers there is always great debate over whether one should use plastic or clay pots. I think the debate is probably lessening now as the best uses of both type of pot have become generally accepted.

Clay pots are the traditional containers for growing alpines. They have several advantages; they are difficult to overwater, they can absorb water through the pot, they keep the plant cool in summer and warm in winter, they have rigid sides and, last but not least, they look better than any other type of container. The disadvantages are that they are heavy, expensive, break, dry out quickly if not attended, sizes are not standard, and are difficult to wash and clean (they were also difficult to find but recently have again become more readily available).

Plastic pots are a relatively recent introduction and, for most practical purposes in the garden, they ousted the traditional clay pots. The have the advantages that they do not dry out so quickly as clays, they are lighter, do not break so easily (at least in theory), they are easier to clean, they come in standard sizes, and they are relatively cheap and easy to purchase. The disadvantages are that it is easy to overwater a plant, drainage is not so good as a clay, it is cold in winter and hot in summer, the sides are flexible, and it looks what it is — plastic.

The thing one has to do is to weigh up the advantages and disadvantages of each type and see what suits you. Many people do strongly feel that alpines grow better in clays but others point out this is just a question of management, particularly watering. Most people are happy to sow seed in plastic pots because here it is important that the soil never dries out and plastic pots can be left outside where they only need attention in dry weather. Many people also grow plants that require a peaty or moister compost; again this is easier to maintain in plastic. As for plants where drainage is important, such as the high alpines, many would rather go for clays. It is possible to vary the composition of the composts used and a grittier, more free-draining compost can be used in plastics to achieve the same results as with a clay. If deep plunging is adopted with wet sand, then clays are preferable; if the pots are stood on gravel then plastics will generally make more sense.

Read all the pros and cons and make up your own mind. Experience will teach you what is preferable in different circumstances. For example, your watering regime will influence your choice; if you are able to water frequently then the clays may be preferable to plastic which may be more suitable if you are only able to water every few days.

Try not to mix the different types of pot on the bench; if you do use both, and most of us do, then keep the plastics in one area and clays in another: it will make watering much easier.

The third type of pot are disposable food containers such as yoghurt cartons, margarine tubs and plastic coffee cups. It is very difficult to know what to say about these. Most alpine growers loathe them and ban them from their plant sales. They feel that it is demeaning to the plant to have to suffer the indignity of such a container, particularly if it has got writing on the side. I must say that I generally agree with this sentiment; plants look much better in proper pots. However, there is the question of cost as well as the fact that the beginner is likely to be starting from scratch with no existing supplies of pots and yet a burning desire to propagate as many plants as he can. Buy proper pots if you are able to afford them, if not use yoghurt cartons (make a drainage hole in the bottom of each one) and change over as soon as you can.

Compost

Here again we enter into the realm of personal choice; everybody has their own favourite recipes. Fortunately, at least in alpines, gardeners have abandoned 'secret' ingredients such as ox-blood and sheep's urine and so on, and stick to basic ingredients.

There are three types of compost: potting, sowing and cutting. At a pinch you can get away with using potting compost for all three operations, but for best results, experience has shown that individual mixtures are best.

Potting composts can be farther subdivided into two types: loam-based and soilless. Most growers prefer loam-based for most situations as it is the freer draining of the two and it is the one we will concentrate on. However before I do so, I ought to say something about the soilless composts. These are basically peat with a chemical fertiliser added to give nutrition and sand to give drainage. Some growers use these where they do not want the compost to dry out too quickly or possibly where the plants like moist, acid conditions; for example the ericaceous plants, such as rhododendrons, appreciate these conditions. Because they hold moisture without much attention, some growers prefer soilless composts for growing seed, but others point out that young plants often have difficulty in making the adjustment between this and a loam-based compost when they are pricked out or potted on.

Personally I have never got on with soilless composts. The greatest difficulty is re-wetting them once the surface has dried out too much. If you do use them, it is important that you add extra drainage in the form of either grit or sharp sand. This will prevent too much moisture being held around the roots of the plant and it will also make it easier to water, particularly if it gets a bit on the dry side.

Soilless composts are very readily available from garden centres and other sources. If you wish to make your own then this can be simply done by adding a fertiliser base, such as Chempak (UK), to peat and sufficient sharp sand or grit to provide adequate drainage. The proportions of the mix are given on the packs. There is also an ericaceous base which is lime-free.

Soil-based composts are by far the most commonly used and the easiest for the beginner to handle. The John Innes Institute ran many trials and came up with a formula that they considered best for growing plants. The main constituents remain the same but the amount of fertiliser is varied giving three strengths known as John Innes (or simply JI) No. 1, No. 2 and No. 3, the second and third having twice and three times respectively as much fertiliser as the first. The main three ingredients are loam, peat and grit or sharp sand. The actual composition is

7 parts (by volume) sterilised loam
3 parts peat
2 parts grit or sharp sand

To each 36 litres (8 gal/1 bushel) of this is added:

21 g ($\frac{3}{4}$ oz) ground chalk
110 g (4 oz) John Innes Base Fertiliser (2 parts (by weight) of hoof and horn meal, 2 parts of superphosphate of lime, 1 part sulphate of potash)

This makes up JI No. 1. For No. 2 and No. 3 the amount of fertiliser is doubled and trebled, but the chalk remains the same. If you are growing ericaceous or other lime-hating plants, then the chalk should obviously be omitted.

John Innes composts can be purchased at any garden centre or you can make them up yourself. The calibre of the composts that are available vary considerably, usually in the quality of the loam. Some safeguard can be obtained by only purchasing that with the John Innes seal on it. Another point to remember is to try always to purchase freshly prepared compost, although the freshness is often difficult to establish. Freshly sterilised loam seems to be more efficacious than stale loam.

For most purposes JI No. 1 is of sufficient strength. Alpines do not want too strong a mix and since they are usually potted on every or every other year, No. 1 will last. In troughs, where the compost will not be replaced for quite a number of years, it is better to use a stronger mix.

It is quite possible to make your own John Innes potting compost. This gives you more control over the ingredients in that you can be sure that you have got a good quality loam and you can use leaf-mould instead of peat if you wish. With your own mixes you are able to leave out the lime and of course you can make it in whatever quantity you like so that it is always fresh. The main difficulty is that it is preferable to sterilise the loam (and leaf-mould if you use it). There is great debate as to whether this is necessary or not; many growers claiming better results with unsterilised materials. However, there is no doubt that many harmful organisms and weed seeds are eradicated. The latest method for sterilising the loam is in a microwave oven when the steam produced will do the job. Electric sterilisers can be purchased for larger quantities.

Getting your John Innes No. 1 is only part of the battle. You now have to turn it into a suitable alpine mixture. Fortunately this is not too difficult; all that is needed is extra grit or coarse sand. Normally one part of JI No. 1 to one part of grit is sufficient, but for even better drainage the proportions may be 1 : 2 or even 1 : 3. For woodland plants it might be advantageous to use 1 part JI No. 1 to 1 part of grit and 1 part of leaf-mould or peat.

The John Innes Institute also produced a recommended formula for a sowing compost:

2 parts (by volume) sterilised loam
1 part peat
1 part grit or sand

To each 36 litres (8 gal/1 bushel) is added:

42 g (1½ oz) superphosphate of lime
21 g (¾ oz) ground chalk

Some growers use this, again with extra grit, but others use the potting compost mixture. The chalk should be omitted for growing seed of ericaceous plants. The thing is that seedlings should be moved on as soon as possible so they do not need too much from the compost except the moisture and physical support. The seed carries its own food supply to get it established.

The third compost is for cuttings and is the easiest to prepare. Here again the medium only needs to provide moisture and support and this is conveniently provided in a 50 : 50 mix of peat and sharp sand (or Perlite and sharp sand). The cuttings should be moved on as soon as they have rooted and therefore there is no need to supply any food.

We have stuck with basic materials which are readily available, but there are increasingly on the market others that can be substituted. For example, Perlite is more water retentive than peat, but does not break down in the same way. My advice is to go down the well tried path of traditional materials and branch out and experiment when you not only have the confidence to do so but the experience which will act as a yardstick for comparing results.

Potting, potting on and repotting

Plants should never be potted into a container that is too large for them. When first potted up seedlings are usually put into 7.5cm (3in) or 9cm (3½in) pots, depending on the size of the plant. If the pot is too large for the root system the soil will retain more moisture than the root can reach and take up. This will not only turn sour but may well rot the roots. With tap-rooted subjects, such as the eryngiums, it is necessary to use deep pots known as 'long toms'. These allow the roots to develop fully without getting wound around the inside of the pot.

With clay pots, which usually have a single drainage hole, and plastic pots with large holes, it is necessary to 'crock'; that is to place a piece of broken pot over the hole to prevent the compost from falling out of the bottom and to preclude its blocking the hole and thus inhibiting drainage. If you are plagued with worms, then it may be necessary to put a piece of plastic or metal mesh over the hole to prevent their entry into the pots. This should not be necessary for pots on a bench, but in a cold frame it is likely that worms will be present. Until recently it was recommended to put a layer of grit at the bottom of the pot to improve the drainage but experiments have shown that this in fact impedes rather than helps with the passage of water. Most people now put the compost directly on the bottom of the pot.

When the pot has been filled and the plant inserted, the compost should be gently firmed and then topdressed with grit. As already mentioned, this grit is very important and serves several purposes: it prevents the compost drying out too fast, it stops the surface becoming hard with constant watering so that water runs off down the side of the pot, it keeps the area around the neck of the plant well-drained, which helps prevent this vulnerable part of the plant from rotting, it inhibits the growth of algae and mosses and facilitates their removal should they form, it provides a good background against which the plant can be displayed to its advantage. Grit is becoming increasingly available from garden centres but another source of supply that many growers use is chicken grit, sold by agricultural merchants and pet stores to poultry owners.

Do not forget to label the pot immediately; if left, the name of the plant and other details can be soon forgotten. I am sure there cannot be an alpine gardener alive who has not kicked himself at some time or other for forgetting the label. Information on labelling is given in Chapter 5.

As the plant grows and fills the pot it becomes important to 'pot on'. This involves removing the plant and putting it into a larger pot containing fresh compost. The point at which to pot on is not always easy to judge. Generally it is when the roots have filled the pot and first show through the drainage hole. In the majority of cases the plants should not be allowed to become pot-bound, that is with their roots twirled round and round the inside of the pot in a terrible tangle. I say in the majority of cases because there are some plants that seem to thrive on being pot-bound; perhaps it is reminiscent of the tight crevices of their native habitat. One famous cyclamen grower never pots on until 'the plants are almost bursting the pots' as they seem to prefer this kind of condition.

Ideally, when potting on, the compost should be moist but neither too dry or too wet, experience will soon show the best state. First gently remove the topdressing from the pot and then with fingers on either side of the plant, hold the pot upside down and give the rim a sharp tap, with a downward movement, on the edge of the bench or table. The plant, with the compost still held around the roots, will then be left in the hand while the pot can be easily removed. The loose soil around the edge of the rootball is removed and any tangled roots gently loosened. It is then placed into the next size of pot. Fresh compost should be used and this can be worked gently around the edge of the plant, tapping the pot on the bench occasionally to firm it down. Do not ram it in or roots will be damaged. The neck of the plant should be at the same level as previously, both of the soil and the rim of the pot. When it is firmly potted, replace the topdressing and then water. Avoid putting the plant straight back into direct sunlight.

Repotting is a slightly different procedure, because here we are dealing with a plant that has reached its largest pot and is repotted back into one of the same size. The plant is knocked out in the same way, the roots are loosened and the old soil is removed. Some people remove anything from a third to two-thirds of the old soil, leaving some intact around the roots, others remove all the compost. The plant is then repotted into a similar-sized pot; it should not be the same pot because it must be clean and there is no time to wash it as the unpotted plant should be out in the drying air for as short a time as possible. Mature plants should be repotted every year if possible, if not then at least every other year.

Watering

To many people this is one of the most difficult aspects of growing alpines. Those thought to have 'green fingers' are those who know when and how to water; it is one of the keys to good growing.

To make things difficult for the beginner it must be said that there is no exact formula; there are so many variables. For example clay pots dry out much quicker than plastic ones as the water evaporates from the porous sides. The composition of the compost also influences the frequency and quantity of watering: a gritty, free-draining one will need more watering than one with more leaf-mould in its make-up. The prevailing weather conditions will affect the regime, even inside an alpine house. Finally, different plants have different requirements, for example many bulbs need very little, if any, water during the summer months, while for many other plants this is the time when their needs are most urgent.

It is important to look into this last aspect carefully and determine which of your plants have a dormant season and when watering should be withheld and when restarted. Use coloured labels in the pots to remind you (and any helper you might have while you are on holiday) what is to be watered when. Plants that should not be over-watered should be potted in clay pots and plunged in sand. The sand can then be kept moist and this will supply sufficient moisture to the plant.

Winter is a difficult time as too much watering can soon kill a plant, but conversely a spell of sunshine can soon dry out the pots under glass without the grower realising it. If the plunge is kept moist throughout the winter this will supply ample moisture without over-watering.

In summer conditions can get very hot in an alpine house unless precautions have been taken (see p. 28). Pots will dry out and plants will transpire heavily using up vast amounts of water. They obviously need regular watering, but keeping the plunge moist and damping other areas such as the concrete floor will help not only to cool the house but to moisten the air reducing the transpiration rate.

Drops of water on foliage can act as lenses and cause scorch marks, so water in the evening on hot sunny days unless the house is well shaded. Another precaution to take is to avoid getting water into the rosettes of plants, some positively dislike it.

Experience will tell you when to water individual pots. The pot and its contents are much lighter when dry. Under the same condition a clay pot will ring when tapped, but make a dull sound when moist. A moist pot standing on a bench will leave a damp ring when lifted, no ring and the pot wants watering. The plant will also indicate when it needs attention, it will show signs of flagging and will become flabby to the touch. When these signs appear the plant should be watered immediately.

It is possible to set up automatic watering systems (see p. 32) which can be used with blocks of plants with similar requirements.

Feeding

This is a vexed question amongst many growers. If you repot regularly with a compost that contains a slow-release fertiliser then there is no need to feed farther. Certainly the use of nitrogenous fertilisers should be restrained as this will produce plants that are far too lush. These will not only look over-blown but make the plant more prone to attack by predators such as aphids. In fast-draining composts any nutrients can be quickly leached out so many growers like to use a liquid feed included in the water once a week or once a fortnight. These are usually a weak solution of a potash feed such as that sold for tomatoes.

Turning pots

One final point that must be made about the care of plants in pots is that if you want to grow perfectly rounded cushion plants that have an even spread of flowers over their surface then it is important to ensure that the plants receive an even distribution of light. Light is rarely even, particularly if shading is used or if there is a building or tree in the vicinity. By turning the pots through 90 degrees every few days, so that the plant is completely rotated every ten days to a fortnight, the plants will get a more even spread of light and the growth will be more regular. This is particularly essential when using lean-to houses.

Raised beds

Raised beds are normally associated with the open garden and we will be looking at them there in a later chapter. However, many growers use them within the alpine house as an alternative or as an adjunct to pot culture; indeed some combine the two in one feature. The basic idea is to provide a certain depth of growing medium, either on the bench or on the ground, in which plants are directly grown, giving them freedom of root-run and a more natural setting than the pot. The compromise is to include plants grown in pots which are plunged to above their rims, giving the appearance of plants growing freely in the bed.

The purpose of raised beds in the alpine house can be twofold. Plants are given the same protection and attention as those grown in pots but they are given a freer root-run and different cultural conditions. The other reason is that the plants are visually more pleasing in a natural setting where rock and pieces of tufa (see Chapter 4) are used to landscape the bed.

The raised bed can be created on a bench or directly on the floor of the house. One of the most important criteria of a bed is that the supports are able to cope with the enormous weight of the moist planting medium and any rocks (plus part of the weight of the gardener who might well lean on it). It should be constructed with sides deep enough to take a depth of compost of at least 20cm (8in) and preferably

A raised bed on the staging of the alpine house

25cm (10in). Some parts can be locally deeper by building it up with walls of stone or tufa. Drainage holes should be provided to prevent stagnant water accumulating in the bottom of the bed. These should be covered with mesh to prevent the compost falling through.

The compost can be the same as is used for potting (see p. 36). Since it will not be changed as frequently as it would if it were in pots, the compost, a base mix of John Innes No. 2 or 3, should contain a slow-release fertiliser. It is possible to get carried away with the grand design and the eventual effect it will make and forget just how much compost will be required to fill the bed. Even a modest one will need quite a lot. If you run short of compost remember that it is better to give the bed the correct depth of material in a smaller space rather than to spread it out into a thinner layer.

The top should be dressed with grit or stone chippings and it can be decorated with rocks or lumps of tufa. These can be purely functional or arranged in a way to give the appearance of a more natural landscape. Tufa should be bedded through the topdressing into the compost so that it can draw up moisture. This can then be drilled and plants grown directly in it (see p. 57).

Beds built on the floor can be more ambitious as there are no problems with weight, indeed in a larger house a rock garden or scree bed can be built using quite large pieces of stone. If the alpine house is in a free-draining area then a part of the bed can be excavated from the floor, thus avoiding the necessity of retaining walls. This means that the grower and observer have farther to bend, but it does get over the problem of having to build the bed up against the glass walls of the house.

If the floor of the alpine house is concrete then walls will have to be built and drainage holes must be accommodated during their construction. The compost mix can be the same as for the bench bed, but the surface dressing can be heavier, using pieces of stone or slate to create the effect of a scree bed. Being built on the ground the bed will be less prone to fluctuations in temperature, but it will be more open to attacks from predators such as slugs. Another disadvantage is that worms will be bound to find their way in, but this does not present such a problem as it does with plants in pots.

While some beds are purely practical in that the grower feels that this is the best way to cultivate a particular plant, others are there purely for the visual effect they create. It is possible to plunge pots with plants in flower to add extra colour or interest to the bed. These should be deeply plunged so that the rim is below the level of the topdressing. Plants should not be left too long in this position as the dressing will be above the usual level and the plant can come to harm when it is put back to its normal position. An eye should be kept on watering, particularly if the pots are plastic as they will be unable to take up much water from the surrounding medium and will need direct watering into the unseen pot.

Maintenance is a simple process with the same kind of attention as one would give to plants in pots, namely attention to watering, removal of dead and broken foliage, feeding and replanting. The watering needs no further comment except that the bulk of compost makes it less likely than pots to dry out suddenly. The rocks will help to provide cool and moist root-runs giving consistency of conditions. Dead material should be removed to help prevent the introduction of disease and predators. Because the soil is not replaced as frequently as that in pots the initial amount of fertiliser should be greater and the bed will need an occasional small amount of slow-release fertiliser or liquid feed. Replacing the whole bed is a major undertaking and not something one would want to undertake each year. Plants

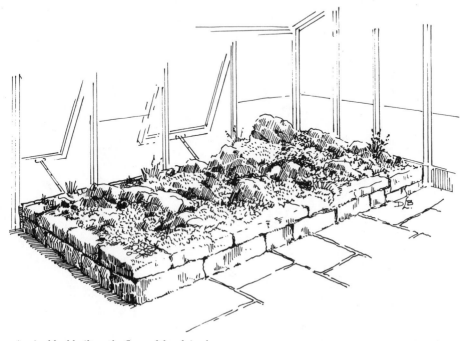

A raised bed built on the floor of the alpine house

43

established in a bed are less happily disturbed than those in pots. If the bed appears to be tired and in need of rejuvenation, it can be replaced a small piece at a time, avoiding those plants that do not like to be disturbed.

If you are using plants that are slightly tender, then a frame covered with two layers of polythene can be constructed to go over the whole or part of the bed during frosty spells. Alternatively newspaper can be laid over it at night. With both types of bed heating wires can be inserted to provide frost protection for some of the more tender plants.

Cold Frames

Cold frames are considered within the chapter on alpine houses because they are in effect low level houses. Most plants that are grown in an alpine house can be grown in a frame, much more cheaply, but with less comfort and ease.

Alpine houses have the advantage over frames in that they can accommodate the grower as well as the plants (particularly important in the winter), they can accommodate taller plants, and the plants are at a level at which it is more easy to attend to them. Frames on the other hand also have advantages: they are much cheaper to produce, they can be more easily built to the grower's own requirements, their volume is smaller so they are easier to keep warm and can be easily covered with insulation material, and it is possible to remove the 'roof' completely in the summer, giving more natural growing conditions.

Frames are basically of two types: those with glass walls and lights (roofs) and those with solid walls and glass lights. The choice depends on what you feel the purpose of your frame to be. If it is just to keep the harsh, cold weather out in the winter then a solid-walled frame is the choice to make, as the glass-walled alternative will need to have the walls insulated to be truly effective. On the other hand if it is all-year-round protection that is needed, for example with bulbs that need to be kept dry in summer, then the glass is better. Similarly if the winter

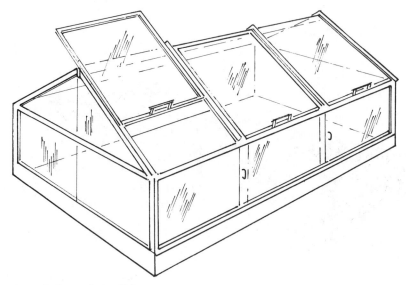

A metal, glass-walled cold frame

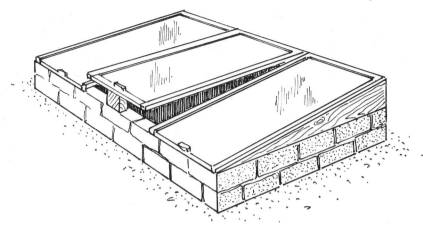

A brick-built cold frame showing the solid walls

protection is mainly to keep out the rain rather than the cold from early flowering plants, then the more light they receive from glass walls the better.

For most purposes a solid-walled frame is adequate and it is the easiest to make. If the ground is free-draining then the frame can be sunk into the ground. This has the advantage of the ground's warmth in the winter and is to a certain extent protected from the wind. The big disadvantage is that it is a long way down when you are trying to introduce or remove pots. Assuming it is above ground, the walls can be built of wood, brick or stone.

Railway sleepers make good walls, they are stable, provide good insulation and take little time to install. Unfortunately they can ooze tar on hot days which inevitably gets on to hands and clothes. Other wooden frames can be constructed by cladding a timber framework with planks or weather boarding. This will make quite a lightweight frame which can be moved to another location if required. The wood should be treated with a preservative but avoid creosote which will give off fumes that are toxic to your plants.

A more solid and non-mobile frame can be made from brick or concrete blocks. To prevent subsidence and cracking, the walls should be built on shallow foundations (10–15cm (4–8in)) of concrete. If thermal blocks are used, it might be sensible to give them a cement rendering otherwise water can enter the holes in the soft material and spall off pieces in the frosts.

In either case the walls should be sloping towards the front of the frame to throw off any water that falls on it, and also allow condensation to run away down the inside of the glass rather than drip back on to the plants. The height need not be too great and is not critical. Enough height should be allowed for the height of a pot, plus the maximum height of the plants it will contain and then some to spare to allow air to circulate. If you only intend to grow cushion plants then the walls can be quite low. To improve the quality of the light in the frame the inside walls can be painted white.

The lights consist of wooden frames with glass inset in them. These are the most difficult parts of the frame to make. It is often possible to find frame lights for sale in a local paper, possibly from a nursery closing down. If you are not too handy this may offer you a reasonably cheap alternative to making your own. They should be long enough to slightly overhang top and bottom to allow water to be shed away from the frame. The lights can be designed such that they only have one large pane of glass or with a central glazing bar and two rows of overlapping glass panes. The former has the advantage that it lets in more light, but the disadvantage that if you break it, all will have to be replaced at great expense, whereas the multiple paned light need only have replaced that piece which was broken.

The frames should be laid out so that there is room to push the lights back behind the frame, making it possible to get at the contents. With smaller frames and lighter lids, it is possible to hinge them at the back and to clip them up in a vertical position. As the lights are left off for most of the summer, there must be space to store them where they will not get trodden on and broken.

Some form of device is useful to prevent the wind sending the lights cartwheeling across the garden. This can take the form of a catch of some sort or weights laid on the frame; catches are the simplest to use.

Shading is as necessary for a frame as it is for an alpine house, more so as there will be less ventilation if the light is on causing the small volume of air to heat up rapidly. It is very easy to make a simple wooden frame over which is stretched some green shading material. These can then be laid over the glass lights, or in hot weather applied instead of the lights. It is important, especially with newly potted up plants, that adequate shading is provided.

The base of the frame can be bare earth on which polythene is laid. If there are any perennial weeds these should be removed as they will find their way round, or through a small hole in, the plastic. The floor should be nearly level but there should be a slight slope to facilitate drainage. The polythene is then covered with a layer of gravel. It can be several centimetres deep if you want to plunge the pots for added winter protection or just a couple of cm (1in) or so if the pots are simply to stand on it. Ashes or sharp sand can be used as an alternative to gravel but these seem to attract green algae and liverwort.

In the main I use my frames as protection from the rain in the winter or during any particularly wet spell elsewhere in the year. Consequently the lights are off for most of the time. When they are on they are very rarely shut up completely; there is usually a block of wood at one or both ends of the light, allowing free circulation of air. In very severe weather or when blowing snow can enter I shut down completely. There are also other times, such as after potting up, when it might be desirable to keep the frames closed, but this should be for as short a time as possible as alpines dislike stagnant air. In cold weather the frames can be covered with sacking or an old carpet to help keep in the warmth.

The watering and the care of the plants is much the same as in the alpine house itself. Keep an eye on the watering; it is easy to believe that because the plants are outside they are getting sufficient moisture from the natural rainfall, a dangerous assumption. Pots in frames do seem prone to capturing passing weed seed and a check should be kept that a forest of weeds is not building up in the pots.

It is quite possible to build plunge or standing beds which are just the shell of the cold frame. Its purpose is to create a neat standing area for pots. When plants are in flower they can be taken into the alpine house for admiration and protection, but for the rest of the year they will be perfectly happy standing out in the fresh air. In a bad winter a polythene light will give sufficient protection from snow, excess rain or cold. However, polythene frames are not as efficient or as permanent as glass.

4 Other Situations

By tradition, and in most lay-people's eyes, alpine gardening is synonymous with rock gardens, or rockeries to use the Edwardian expression. If the plants are grown in pots then the alpine house is seen to come into its own, but there are many other ways of growing alpines. Some are dictated by convenience or economics, while others provide the best growing conditions for the plants in a garden situation (the optimum growing conditions surely must be in the wild). This chapter is going to look at some of the alternatives.

Raised Beds

In the last chapter the use of raised beds in the alpine house was discussed, but it is in the open garden where this form of alpine gardening is mainly practised. Here they can consist of no more than a few square metres of a hollow wall on the edge of a patio or a much larger, specially constructed bed.

A raised bed is simply a structure which supports a quantity of compost, above ground level, suitable for growing alpines. The idea behind it is that being above the ground, it is both free-draining and easier to appreciate and tend to the plants. Since they are often made of stone or brick walls, in a more formal garden, they are easier to accommodate than a rock garden.

Siting

There is more scope in siting a raised bed than a rock garden. It is still best to avoid shady areas, unless you want to grow shade-loving plants. Overhanging trees will cause a nuisance from the drip of rain from the leaves and the thirst and hunger of their pervasive root system. Anywhere in the open, sunny situation will do. The drainage of the underlying soil is not critical as the bed will be raised above soil level, leaving the plants' roots well clear of stagnant water. However, it should not be built on an area where there is lying water as this will percolate up into the bed.

The bed is not restricted to being built on soil, it can be built on concrete or any other solid surface as long as excess water can escape from the bottom of the bed through holes left in the wall.

It can be used as an attractive feature on or at the edge of a patio or terrace, or as an edging to a path or drive. A popular place is alongside paths that are constantly used. This allows the plants to be regularly admired or checked to see if there are any problems. They can equally be built on the edge or in the middle of lawns.

In less formal areas of the garden they can be constructed in utility areas amongst the frames and alpine house, either as self-contained units or in conjunction with some other feature. The ends of some of my frames abut the main path at 45 degrees and I have utilised the triangular spaces thus created by building small raised beds. I have a similar feature along the back of the alpine house.

A raised bed can be used as a decorative feature

Shape

The shape is entirely up to the builder, the plants will not mind at all. It can be square, rectangular, curved, circular or triangular. In more formal parts of the garden the design should be dictated by how it fits with the overall appearance. In utility areas or in gardens where the appearance is of little consequence, then rectangular beds are the ones usually constructed. In cold areas or if tender plants are grown it can be a good idea to cover the bed with a polythene frame during severe weather. The construction of the frames is much easier if the beds are of a regular shape.

Structure

The height can be as high as you like, but there are several things to consider before you go mad and build one 1.2m (4ft) from the ground. First there is the question of materials; this will use a lot of brick or stone, but more importantly it will use an awful lot of compost. You will have to dig a corresponding hole somewhere else if your soil is suitable or buy it in, which will come expensive, particularly as you will also need peat and grit. If you are planting alpines they will be using only the top 25cm (10in) or so. When such a tall bed is built and filled, the soil, however much you ram it in, will inevitably subside and you will be topping it up for many years, disturbing the plants each time. The other point is that the height of the structure will mean that it will need to be very strong, possibly with buttresses. So think twice about tall beds.

The best height is between 25 and 60cm (10–24in), the ultimate height being determined partly by aesthetic reasons (i.e. the best looking height) and partly by the material used: if you are using old railway sleepers then it should be either one or two sleepers high, not one and a half, which would require the laborious task of cutting one down the middle.

The material can be whatever you like: stone, brick and wood are the usual ones. Out of sight, or if the aesthetics are of little consequence, materials such as railway sleepers or concrete can be used. Railway sleepers can ooze tar in hot weather, which inevitably gets on to hands and clothes. Planks of wood can be used but they quickly rot and are far from satisfactory. Logs can also be used, but these should be straight so that there are no gaps between them from which compost can trickle. They are much better suited to raised peat beds, where plants can be planted in the cracks (see p. 67). Elm is a good wood to use if you can still find it after the recent disasters that have befallen it. If kept damp it is slow to rot (hollowed-out elm was used as water pipes in days gone by). Keep an eye on wooden raised beds as the walls can suddenly give way spilling the contents everywhere. Wood, of course, can be treated with preservative but do not use creosote as the fumes given off (continuing for many years) will kill off any alpines you plant.

Stone or brick are the more usual materials from which raised beds are constructed. It is easier to use stone blocks, either genuine or reconstituted, which are regular in shape. They should be bonded together with cement; it is possible to lay them like a dry-stone wall, but this is very difficult to construct properly and, as the soil-mix settles within it, the whole can burst open. If it is attempted then the walls should slope slightly in towards the middle of the bed, adding the soil-mix (see below) as the walls are built up. Every so often a longer stone should be laid end-on so that it protrudes out into the soil-mix, acting like an anchor. Ram the soil-mix in firmly as you go. Cement bonded walls should be vertical and filled when the cement is dry.

If bricks are used the colour should match or be sympathetic to those of the house or any other brick structure in the vicinity. It is a wise precaution to ensure that the bricks are frost-proof.

Small gaps should be left at the base of the wall to ensure that water does not get trapped inside. Other small gaps can be left in the walls through which plants can grow. These should not be too large as they will weaken the structure. Naturally it is difficult to force a plant into a narrow space, but it is very easy to blow seed into such a crevice and let nature take its own course.

Gaps must be left in walls to provide for drainage

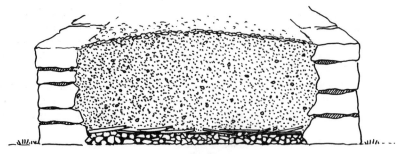

A cross-section through a raised bed

Filling the bed

The base of the bed should be lined with broken clay pots and other crocks (rubble or stones will do) to allow any excess of water to drain away. Broken tiles or slates can cover these to prevent its being clogged with compost.

The compost itself is the same mixture as prescribed for the rock garden (p. 15). Because it will not be disturbed for a number of years it is best to use the stronger mix based on John Innes No. 3 using a slow-release fertiliser. Tread or otherwise firm the compost into the bed. It is best to hump it up over the level of the walls as it will soon sink. And the deeper the bed the farther it will sink. If you can bear to wait, the bed can be left a couple of months before planting to allow for this shrinkage. It is possible, for example, to construct the bed in autumn and plant it up in the spring, having made good any drop in level.

The surface can now be dressed with gravel or stone chippings. Rocks or lumps of tufa can be embedded in it both to enhance its appearance and to give the plants protection and a cool root-run.

Plants grown in pots can be planted out at any time as long as hot, dry or windy weather is avoided, but generally spring is the best time. Scrape the topdressing back and dig a hole, spreading the plant's roots as it is put in. Firm and replace the grit dressing. Water in and label. Not everybody likes to see labels on their raised beds, and it is possible to either bury them (remembering where you put them of course!) or draw a map of the bed on which you keep your records. Always put the label in the same place relative to the plant; to the top right for example. This will tell you roughly where the plant is if it dies back underground every year.

Maintenance

If constructed properly and weed-free compost was used, little maintenance will be required. Weeds, obviously, should be removed as soon as they appear and plants tended to in the normal way, removing dead and broken material for example. Early each year a small amount of general fertiliser can be applied to the surface, avoiding getting it on the plants. Nutrients will be leached out of the free-draining soil so they must be replaced. At the same time the grit or chipping dressing should be checked and topped up if necessary (it slowly works its way down into the bed, often leaving the top bare).

Watering is very important. Since the bed is likely to be in a sunny and possibly windy position it will lose moisture quite fast. It should be watered regularly and barely a week or ten days should go by without its receiving either rain or water from a sprinkler. Give the bed a good dose, water from a watering can is rarely sufficient if used over a large area.

There should be no necessity to replace the soil for many years but if plants start looking tired or sick then it is time to rejuvenate it. This can be done by taking all the soil out, or by doing a portion at a time. If you were methodical enough, you could replace a fifth of the soil every year for example.

Scree Beds

Screes are the accumulation of loose stones, at the foot of rocky areas. Those on the lower slopes are relatively stable, but higher up they are often constantly on the move. For obvious reasons it is better to emulate the former rather than the latter in the garden.

The whole essence of the scree bed is that it is very free-draining. They can be constructed by having a layer of compost covered by a depth of gravel, chippings or small stones. The compost should be a mixture of 50 per cent grit, and 25 per cent each of loam and leaf-mould or peat.

They can take various forms in the garden. A raised bed can even be thought of as a scree particularly if it contains extra grit, giving it sharp drainage. Part of the rock garden can be adapted, especially if it can be arranged that the scree appears to be pouring from between two large rocks, fanning out towards the viewer. This has the advantage of being on a slope, increasing the drainage. The third possibility is just to spread a layer of gravel or stones on top of ordinary garden soil. One of the best known scree gardens was in Kent where the owner placed a 25cm (10in) layer of gravel on top of his sticky Wealden clay. He planted directly into the gravel and the roots travelled down to find nourishment and water in the clay. The only difficulty was that it was awkward to move plants once their toes were down in the clay. Other gardens have been similarly constructed using large stones, including beach pebbles. Although it worked on the clay, it is preferable to build a scree bed of this type on a better soil, certainly a better drained soil.

Planting is direct into the scree, adding extra soil to make certain that the rootball has contact with the compost or the soil in the bed. When planting a scree bed it is essential to see that the plants do not suffer a shortage of water until they have established themselves.

A scree bed pouring from between rocks in the rock garden

A planted trough

Sinks and troughs

One of the good things about alpines is that you can vary the size of the garden according to the space available, size of your pocket, time available and your physical ability. On the one hand you can create a large rock garden (the biggest that I have seen in a private garden was 5,000sq m (1¼ acres), all maintained by the owner himself) or you can have just a trough or sink of a square metre (sq yd). The small size of the trough makes it an ideal way of gardening for the elderly and the handicapped, particularly as it can be raised, making it possible to attend it from a wheelchair.

There are very many plants that will happily adapt to life in a trough. With the use of judiciously placed pieces of rock, a wide variety of habitats can be created. In effect a trough can become a miniature rock garden.

Siting

There is no difference in placing a trough than any other of the features that carry alpine plants. An open situation with plenty of sun and circulating air, but not draughts or strong winds. Avoid overhanging trees and bushes as these will cause drips in wet weather which the plants will not tolerate. They can be placed on any solid surface, of which terraces or patios are a strong favourite. They can be placed on lawns but this presents terrible problems with mowing. It is particularly difficult with hypertufa troughs (see below) where the coating can become very easily cracked and broken off by the mowing machine.

Structure

The traditional (or at least traditional since the 1920s) trough is one hewn from a single lump of stone. In a previous existence they were usually used for providing water for cattle and other livestock. These have a natural look about them that is very appealing; the surfaces are usually rough and carry a patina of age. Unfortu-

52

nately they are getting very difficult to find and, when they can be located, very expensive. Some enterprising firms have started manufacturing troughs for garden use, but like so many products aimed at this market, they look cheap and rather nasty in spite of being made from a solid block of natural stone.

There are, however, two alternatives: adapt an existing sink or make your own. Until recently it was very easy to obtain glazed sinks that were being taken out of houses to be replaced with stainless steel ones. Unfortunately this source is now beginning to dry up, although they can still be found with a bit of effort (the stainless steel ones are unlikely to be of much use once their time is done!). These white sinks are hideous in themselves but can be adapted to make a reasonable imitation of the real trough. The magic ingredient is a mixture called hypertufa.

Hypertufa is a simple mixture that when dry resembles real tufa (see below) both in appearance and function. In the case of sinks, its function is purely cosmetic; it transforms the sink into a trough. The mixture is equal proportions of cement, sand and sifted peat, mixed with water to the normal consistency of cement: a thick cream. The outside of the sink is thoroughly cleaned and when dry a thin covering of contact adhesive is applied. A 2cm (¾in) layer of the hypertufa mixture is then placed completely over the outside and over the top and down the inside to below what will be the soil level. The mixture must not dry out too quickly, particularly in hot weather, otherwise it will crack and fall off, so cover it with a damp sack. This will allow it to cure slowly. When dry either a coating of milk or liquid cow manure applied to the surface will speed up the process of aging by encouraging lichen and mosses to form. The finished trough is likely to be heavy, so if possible carry out the work with the sink in its final position.

One advantage that sinks have over troughs is that they are bound to have a drainage hole. With troughs it may be necessary to drill one or two through the bottom. If you make your own troughs then these can be allowed for in the construction.

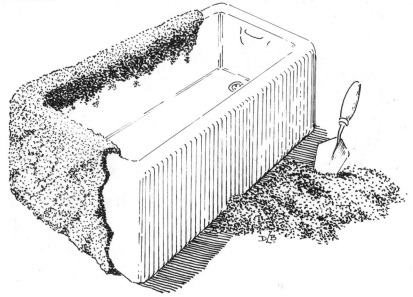

A sink in the process of being covered with hypertufa

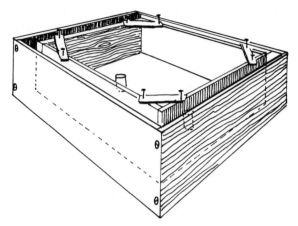

Wooden formers ready for making a concrete or hypertufa trough

Making your own troughs is not as difficult as it sounds. The easiest way is to cast one using the hypertufa mixture mentioned above. Having decided the size, wooden shuttering is made for the outside and inside of the trough. Wooden pegs are placed in the positions of the drainage holes and chicken wire is inserted to act as reinforcement. Hypertufa is then poured between the shuttering. The advantage of wooden shuttering is that it can be used again and you can produce as many troughs as you want for yourself and your friends. A cheaper way but one that can only be used once is to use two cardboard boxes. One should obviously be smaller than the other, allowing about 4–5cm (1½–2in) space between them. The base of the larger is filled with a 5cm (2in) layer of hypertufa and drainage pegs (to be removed when the cement is set) placed in position. The inner box is placed on top of this and filled with earth to prevent it collapsing when the intervening spaces are filled with

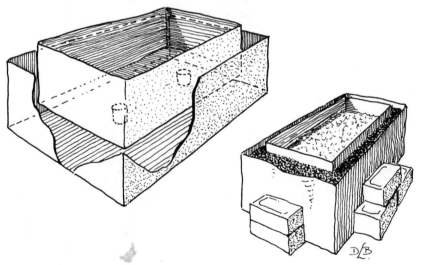

Cardboard boxes used as a non-renewable former for a concrete or hypertufa trough

the hypertufa. Again it should be covered with a wet sack to prevent it cracking. After a couple of days the cardboard can be torn away but the sacking should remain until the sink has thoroughly dried.

Both the hypertufa-covered sink and the hypertufa trough should be allowed to stand and weather before they are filled with compost and planted.

Installation

Troughs of any type are extremely heavy, particularly when filled with compost. This has several safety implications. Be careful how you move them; it is easy to cause a back injury. Get help if necessary and be certain to position the trough before you fill it, which will lighten the burden considerably. Another aspect of safety is stability. If it is intended to raise the trough from the ground, for use by the elderly or the handicapped from a wheelchair for example, be absolutely certain that its support is both stable and strong enough. This cannot be overstressed. Brick or concrete block piers built on a solid base are the safest.

The question of supports at a lower level is a vexed one. To help with drainage and to give the trough a better appearance it is a good idea to lift it a brick's height or so from the ground. The disadvantage is that all kinds of rubbish, leaves, sticks, paper and other detritus can collect there making it a haven for slugs and other pests. The best solution is to raise it up 45cm (18in) or so which removes the problem or have it at the lower level and to resolve to keep it clean.

If possible put it on a solid base such as paving stones. Normally, troughs are placed on a terrace or patio either in isolation or with another one or two troughs, but it is possible to remove a couple of slabs from the terrace and have low plants growing around the base of the trough. This softens the edges and makes the whole thing look a great deal more attractive.

Some sinks and troughs have bottoms sloping towards the drainage hole if there is one. If it has a flat bottom, make certain that it is level or slopes in such a way as to ensure that water will find its way to the hole. As with all aspects of alpine growing, drainage is all important.

Once the trough is in position it can be filled. First a layer of broken crocks or rubble is put in the bottom. If the trough is deep enough it is traditional to put inverted turves on top to prevent the compost from getting into the crocks and impeding drainage. They should of course contain no perennial weeds such as couch grass! Now it is possible to use special polythene which allows the free passage of water, after which the trough is ready to be filled with compost. The mixture can again be based on a John Innes potting compost (see p. 37). No. 3 is best as it will not be changed for several years and a slow-release fertiliser is advisable. Extra grit is added to the JI mixture. Make certain that the compost is well firmed down and hump the surface slightly to allow for the inevitable subsidence.

Lumps of rock can be bedded in the trough, partly to enhance its appearance and partly to provide differing habitats for the plants. Sun-lovers can be on the sunny side of the rocks which will also reflect back the heat and shade-lovers can be on the opposite sides; more peat or leaf-mould being added to the compost for those that favour a moister position. Crevices can be created for those that prefer to live in a more vertical position. If the trough is home-made it is possible to leave holes in the side through which crevice plants can be grown, but be certain that these do not weaken the structure.

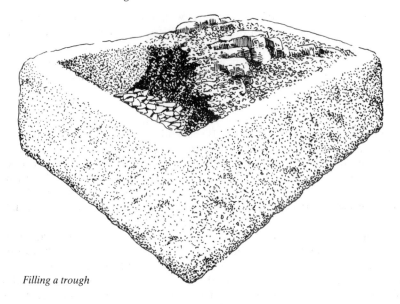

Filling a trough

A topdressing of gravel or stone chippings that are sympathetic to the type of rock used is applied and then the trough is ready for planting. If you are completely planting it straightaway, then it might be easier to leave the topdressing until after the plants are in position. Indeed the plants and the rocks can be put in at the same time which will make it much easier to get the former in the right positions.

The range of plants that can be grown in a trough is enormous. If small plants are chosen even a moderately sized one can grow a score or more. It adds to the height and overall appearance if shrubs, even conifers, are used. Trailing plants, such as phloxes, will soften the edge of the trough. A list of suitable plants is given in Appendix I.

Tufa

Tufa is a remarkable substance; it looks like stone yet it is extremely light (when dry), soft (when young) and porous. It can be easily drilled and plants will happily grow in the holes provided, some better than in any other situation.

Tufa is formed when water carrying minerals, mainly of calcium and magnesium carbonates, passes slowly through moss or some other organic plant material. The minerals are deposited on the moss, rather like scale in a kettle, the original moss dies, forming a new layer on the surface which in due course is covered with minerals and so on as the rock is slowly built up. Since it is formed on the strands of moss there are plenty of air holes which make the rock extremely porous. It is very slow to form but large deposits have built up and can be found in many countries.

Large quantities can be bought directly from the quarries which advertise regularly in specialist alpine journals. Smaller quantities are available from specialist alpine nurseries and, increasingly, from general garden centres. When purchasing tufa be certain to go after a dry spell of weather rather than a wet one or you will be paying for all the rain the tufa has absorbed, as it is priced according to the weight you buy. It is very light when dry but can more than double its weight when wet. Go and select the pieces yourself, do not order it as the size, shape and general appearance varies considerably. Before you go to buy get some idea from the site the size of the piece you require.

Freshly 'mined' tufa has a pale creamy white appearance but this will soon change to a mature grey. It will also be very soft, again this will change as the tufa hardens with age so that eventually, after many years, it will be unworkable. While buying a large piece, smaller pieces can also be acquired for use in troughs or raised beds. Tufa dust can also be purchased for mixing into special composts for one or two plants that prefer it.

Installation

Being light, a large lump of tufa can be brought home in the car. Most of the types of plants that are likely to be grown in it are high alpines which prefer full light or just a little bit of shade, which can be provided by planting them on the shady side of the lump: so the ideal situation is going to be in full sunlight.

It is no good just putting the lump down on a paved terrace or patio. The plants derive their moisture from within the rock, which must be kept moist. Sticking up in the open the rock is prone to quick drying in the sun and wind unless it can be kept supplied with water. The best way to do this is to ensure that part of the lump is below ground level where it can suck up moisture from the surrounding soil. Therefore if you want to use it as a specimen lump on a patio then one or more of the slabs will have to be removed and the tufa dug into the ground. Any space between the tufa and the surrounding slabs can be filled with gravel. Several lumps of tufa can make fine features in an area of gravel, perhaps also containing a few troughs. Indeed in a very small garden, the whole space can be turned over to growing alpines in troughs and tufa where as many plants can be grown as in a large garden with a rock garden. They will be smaller of course but none the less just as attractive and will give as much pleasure.

A similar pattern occurs wherever the tufa is used. In a trough for instance or in a raised bed, part of the lump will need to be buried to make good contact with the compost. Try to overcome any impulse to think that it is a waste of good money to buy stone and then bury it, the part below ground will be money well spent.

The other thing that can be done with tufa is on a much bigger scale: a tufa cliff. The most famous of these was created by the Editor of the Alpine Garden Society *Bulletin* in Birmingham. This basically was a raised bed 45cm (18in) high at the front and 1.5m (5ft) high at the back on which was piled large lumps of tufa to form a cliff 7.6m (25ft) long. The whole thing was covered in by a bus shelter giving ideal growing conditions for many difficult alpine plants, including notoriously difficult *Jankaea heldreichii*. It is big enough to take quite large plants including shrubs. Being under cover it does need watering to top up the tufas's reserves. I have also seen a similar cliff in Czechoslovakia, this time built in the open and in the form of a short walk-in valley dug into a sloping garden. This gives a wide variety of sunny and shady positions, some of which, particularly at the foot of the cliff, were quite damp. Here, besides the jankaea, were primulas and that most difficult of plants *Eritrichium nanum* all growing quite happily. Elsewhere in this garden there was a large lump of tufa on which an *Eritrichium nanum* plant had been growing for seven years in the open alongside a *Viola delphinantha* which had been there for four years; both have no cover in winter other than snow. Both these plants are very difficult to grow satisfactorily for any length of time in any other fashion.

Do not be surprised if pieces spall off during the first few winters until the rock has weathered and hardened. In deep frosts the water within the tufa can become frozen and the expansion will force off small pieces. Any such losses can be philosophically accepted as what happens to rock in the mountains when scree is formed!

Planting

Many plants will grow very happily in tufa, including those such as *Campanula zoysii* and *Physoplexus comosa* (formerly *Phyteuma comosum*), which can be difficult in pots or open beds. Although the tufa contains calcium it seems to be locked up in some way and, strangely, it is quite possible to grow many lime-haters in it.

Fortunately for the first few years after quarrying, tufa is still relatively soft and it is possible to make holes in it either with a drill and a large bit or with a hammer and chisel. In fact it is soft enough to gouge one out with an old screwdriver. A hole is required about 2.5cm (1in) in diameter and about 5–7.5cm (2–3in) deep. It should be sloped slightly downwards so that the plant and any compost is not washed out. It can be very difficult to get a plant into this hole, particularly if you try it with a mature plant having a large rootball. It is best to attempt it with a young plant from which all the soil has been removed from the roots. Gently wrap the roots in a wet paper handkerchief or tissue, forming a long sausage. This is then introduced into the hole and compost gently eased in and firmed around the roots. The plant should be kept moist until it is established. The roots will quickly grow through the paper. Alternatively, the roots can be left free and gently eased into the hole using a stick or widger as a guide.

Another method is to fill the hole with compost and plant seed direct into this. Once established many plants will self-sow directly into the tufa.

Although tufa acts as a large sponge, it must not be ignored and allowed to dry out. Watering directly on to the tufa can have little effect as most of the water will run off, but if the soil in which the tufa is embedded is kept moist, capillary action will do the rest by drawing water up into the lump. No other maintenance is required except to take out any weeds that chance to seed into it.

Dry stone walls

Houses in many parts of Britain are blessed by having stone walls surrounding, or partly surrounding, their gardens. In others it is possible to build such a feature within the garden, either as a screen, or for supporting a bank or raised bed. All these, particularly the last two, make ideal places to grow plants, even on the shady side where such plants as *Ramonda* will be extremely happy.

Free-standing stone walls are an art in themselves and this is not the place to go into their construction even if I were able to. If you have one you are very lucky, if not then get a professional to construct one for you or go into the subject very thoroughly before you start. It is possible to make a 'pseudo' dry stone wall by building a stone wall with mortar, but keeping it well back so that it cannot be seen in the joints.

Retaining walls or walls built up against banks for effect are much easier to construct as you have the support against which you can build. If it is being built for the sole purpose of growing alpines rather than a vital support of sliding or crumbling ground then this is well within the scope of an amateur. Low walls will

A dry stone wall

need no foundations, but above 30cm (1ft) or so foundations will be needed to prevent subsidence and the whole lot crashing down. The wall should be built slightly away from the bank, backfilling as you go with a free-draining compost into which the plants will thrust their toes. This should be well firmed down and topped up when it subsides, which it inevitably will. The wall should be sloped backwards for stability (not too steeply though or the bottom will bulge and burst out). Individual stones should also slope back into the bank not only for stability but also to ensure that water runs back into the compost. Every so often a long stone should be placed at right angles to the wall, going back into the soil to act as a stabiliser and anchor. Keep the crevices as small as possible between the stones. This is mainly to prevent soil being washed out from behind the wall, but many of the plants will prefer a tight crevice into which to grow. Walls around raised beds have already been covered (see p. 48).

Plants or rooted cuttings can be put into the wall as it is built or they can be pushed into the crevices in the wall using the same techniques as mentioned earlier for planting in tufa (see p. 58). With a free-standing dry stone wall there will be little into which the plants can root, so compost should be pushed into the crevices. In dry areas these walls can get very dry and the plants may need extra water outside the rainy season.

Rather than plant the walls it is possible to blow seed into the crevices and let nature take its own course. *Erinus alpinus* is an ideal candidate for this and although not a long-lived plant, once established it will continue to self-sow. Obviously anything which is too robust, such as shrubs or tap-rooted plants that are likely to burst open the wall with their roots, should be avoided.

Alpine lawns

Here we are possibly entering the realms of fantasy. The idea behind alpine lawns is to emulate the alpine meadows which entrance so many visitors to the mountains every spring. Unfortunately this is one of the most difficult of alpine conditions to create in the garden. Many have attempted it and most have failed. To ensure it works entails a great deal of effort and attention, far more than most people can devote. Unless you have plenty of time or are imbued with the spirit of adventure, it can only be recommended that you grow your plants in conventional beds where there is more than a fair chance they will flourish.

Those who want to press ahead have a choice of two types of alpine lawn: one is an imitation of the meadow with grass and plants intermingled, the other is more of an alpine carpet where spreading alpines intermesh and grass is banished.

The former has become very popular in recent years in the form of 'wild flower gardening', where meadows are created using native wild flowers either grown in lawns that have been allowed to become unkempt, by letting the whole garden go wild or in a more controlled way by sowing special grass and wild flower seed together. The problem that has soon become apparent to gardeners attempting this is that the grass and weeds soon take over and choke out the flowering plants. Now if this happens with native plants that to a certain extent are used to putting up with our own thugs, it can be imagined that smaller alpine plants stand no chance at all in the struggle.

The only way to succeed is to remove all the coarse grasses or weeds either by killing off the lot thoroughly with weedkiller and then sowing short growing, soft grasses or constantly mowing the grass for a number of years so that the coarser grasses give up, leaving the soft ones. The lawn can then be planted with the bulbs and spring flowers that you desire. It is sensible to only include plants that all flower and seed at the same time; if they are spread throughout the year then there will be no chance of cutting the grass and disaster will ensue. The grass should be cut in late July or August after the plants have seeded and then once or twice more before the end of the year. Any coarse grasses or weeds should be removed. To add to authenticity a few rocky outcrops can be included in the grass; it looks better but makes it difficult to mow.

This works more easily on chalk downland where the grass is not so vigorous as on the heavier soils. Often rabbits help to keep the swarth tightly cropped — the only time when rabbits are welcome in the garden. An ideal site for such a lawn is linking one rock garden with another, or to act as a transition with the rest of the garden.

The other type of alpine lawn includes no grass in it at all. The plot must be thoroughly cleared of any weeds, preferably leaving it for a while after preparation to check that there are no pieces of perennial weeds left in it. Tough, mat-forming plants can then be planted, usually in groups of three or more plants. They should quickly cover the ground and fight it out where their individual territories meet. It is essential to remove any weeds or grass that subsequently appear. However clean the ground was when you started there is bound to be quite a lot of weed seed (and litter) blown on to the bed.

The classic plant to use in such a bed is thyme. There are two such beds at Sissinghurst Castle in Kent, which are composed entirely of different types of thyme, all of differing shades of pink. It looks truly beautiful, but, as the gardeners will tell you, it takes a lot of maintenance to keep it looking so. Unlike a true lawn it needs to be taken apart every few years and replanted. The centre of the plants get old and die back leaving bald patches for weeds to colonise.

This type of lawn is not restricted to plants that all flower at the same time, there can be something of interest throughout the year. Spreading plants can be underplanted with bulbs. Any of the plants that can make themselves a nuisance in a conventional rock garden or raised bed can be used. Plants such as sedums, acaena, arenaria, hypsela and the creeping campanulas. More are listed in Appendix I.

Patio and paved gardens

Many gardens are so small that they have no space for a conventional garden. In a small area it is even impossible to have a lawn; it would be difficult to mow and besides there is no room for a shed to keep the mower, and the decision may have been taken to pave the whole area. Similarly in larger gardens it might be decided to have a paved area for sitting on or simply as a contrast to the cultivated part. As an alternative to the brash plastic urns of pelargoniums and petunias it is possible to create an alpine garden in such an environment.

The most obvious way is to use troughs or build raised beds on the patio itself. Raised beds can be created by building double walls along the edge of the paving, and then filling and planting it as described earlier in this chapter (see p. 47).

This style of gardening has much to commend it when space is limited. A large range and variety of plants can be grown, which would be impossible in a small space with conventional bedding and perennial plants. And if it were they would tend to clash and look too busy: their attraction lies in using drifts in association with one another. Many different alpines can be used, broken perhaps by the use of rock, without its having the same jarring on the senses as does, for example, a mass of different bedding plants.

It also gives the elderly or handicapped gardener a whole garden to deal with but on a miniature scale; a scale with which he or she can cope.

But troughs and raised beds are not the only possibility in the paved garden. Admittedly they are not so easy for the elderly as they are at ground level, but it is possible to plant in the cracks between the paving slabs, or even remove the odd slab and plant the area exposed.

When laying the slabs, some of the joints can be left empty and can subsequently be filled with compost. Rooted cuttings can be eased down into holes in this and watered in. Another way is to sow seed directly into these crevices and let them germinate and grow on.

Plants used in this situation should be reasonably tough as they inevitably will be walked upon and brushed sharply with a broom when the paved area is swept. Thyme is a good example of a plant that will take this treatment. It has the added advantage that it is aromatic and will smell sweetly when the leaves are bruised by someone treading on them. Another tough plant is the acaena, but do not plant this if you have the habit of walking about bare-footed as the burs can be quite painful.

The other possibility is to remove whole paving slabs and replace them with a miniature garden. This takes a little more preparation because the underlying soil must be free-draining. If the patio was laid directly on to a heavy clay soil, any hole that is dug to fill with compost will act as a sump and fill with water. If these conditions do prevail then drainage will have to be arranged from any such planting holes to a soakaway some distance off.

Assuming the soil is free-draining and that any surface water from the patio itself is carried off to a drain, then a hole should be dug to a depth of about 25cm (10in) and filled with the same mixture as would be used in a rock garden or raised bed (see

p. 15). As always it should be free-draining. It can be topped off with a couple of rocks and given a good mulch of gravel or stone chippings. When planted it can look like a very attractive miniature landscape.

There is no limit to the plants used to furnish it. Dwarf conifers or other shrubs can be used to give it height and a more structural framework. Any plants that are used in a raised bed or trough are suitable.

Maintenance is the same as for a trough. Keep watered in dry weather but the surrounding slabs will provide a cool root-run and will help to conserve moisture so that it can possibly be left for a longer period without water. Replant with new soil either in whole or in part every five years or when the plants begin to look tired and in need of rejuvenation. A light feed of a general fertiliser can be given every spring. There is a tendency for such a low level bed to attract litter and leaves blown along by the wind. Keep the bed free of these and any other detritus, not only for the sake of appearance but also for hygiene reasons; it will help to prevent attacks by pests and diseases.

As an alternative a paving slab can be removed and a piece of tufa part buried in the soil and then surrounded with gravel. This can make a very attractive feature. For a more modernistic garden large lumps of tufa can be supported on vertical steel columns at varying heights up to 1.8m (6ft) or even hung on stout chains. This goes against all the normal principles of using tufa but I saw both being done very successfully in a botanic garden of all places, where summer rainfall was quite slight. They must have somebody who waters the rock thoroughly every day.

Bulb Frames

Nearly all alpine gardeners grow some bulbs, but there are those for whom it is their great passion and they grow these almost to the exclusion of anything else. If one stops to think about it, it seems strange that bulbs come within the sphere of alpine gardening because many of them come from hot desert regions, but it is because of this that they have to be given special treatment.

Many, many bulbs can be grown in the open garden; in the rock garden, raised bed, trough or even alpine lawn. Some bulbs need a little more attention and it is possible to grow these in the alpine house where they are protected against the extremes of the weather and where they can be seen more intimately when they are in flower. But if the intention is to grow a lot of bulbs then a bulb frame becomes advisable.

A bulb frame is just a framework in which the sides and top are glass, sitting on top of what in effect is a raised bed. Its function is to protect the bulb, not so much from the winter cold as from the summer rain.

In the wild, most bulbs that the alpine gardener is interested in appear in the spring and, once seeding has taken place, they disappear below ground again. During summer they are dried off and given a baking by the sun. In a maritime climate, bulbs are given little chance of this ripening process because of the irregular bursts of rain. The only way to emulate the bulb's natural home is to cover it with glass, to keep the rain out and the heat in.

One must not be too dismissive about the role of the frame in winter. Many of the bulbs that it protects are on the tender side and the extra protection from the cold, albeit slight, is welcomed by the bulbs. It is also necessary in a very wet winter to keep the excess water away from the bed.

A bulb frame is a very simple structure. The base is just a raised bed with walls of

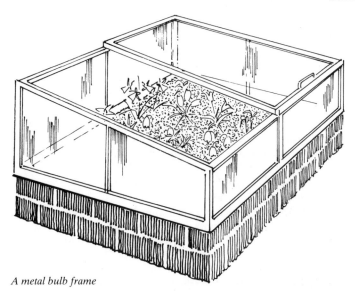

A metal bulb frame

about 25cm (10in) from the ground. They can be made of any material, brick, stone, concrete blocks or railway sleepers. Many of the more 'luxurious' frames are 75cm (2½ft) from the ground, which makes it much easier to attend to the bulbs, and indeed to see them. It would be terribly expensive and unnecessary to fill all of this height with compost; piers 45cm (18in) or so can be built to support a corrugated plastic or iron sheet on which the compost is placed. It can equally be filled with rubble, this being covered with something that will not allow the compost to trickle through, again plastic sheeting would work.

On the top of this base is placed a frame with glass sides and roof. Most people buy this ready-made, normally with an aluminium frame and sliding glass panels, the glass can also be removed. It is possible to make your own, especially if you want them to fit a particular space or of a certain size. The frame can be made of wood or aluminium extrusion can be purchased from specialised outlets. It is sensible to cover the frame on all sides with glass although there is no necessity to have it all on at any one time. If possible it is useful to have the panes on the top to overlap the eaves slightly to throw any water, from a sudden downpour, clear of the sides which may be open.

Because some of the panes will be removed or at least opened, it does allow cats to enter and use the dry bed as a luxury litter tray. Similarly birds can enter and nip off the flowers, so it is a wise precaution to make up some simple frames covered with wire mesh, to place over the openings.

If the frame is on bare earth then a fine-meshed chicken wire-netting should be placed over the ground before filling. This is to prevent mice and moles burrowing their way in. Mice will eat the bulbs, moles will only be after worms, but they will cause a great disturbance; not only will bulbs become mixed up, but many will be left with their roots dangling, without moisture, into the mole's run. While the wire prevents their entrance from underneath, it is more difficult to stop them coming in over the walls. The higher the bed the better the chance, certainly from moles.

There is no way of keeping earthworms out from those frames resting on the ground. The earth can be covered with a perforated plastic sheet which will allow the water through and the worms out, but they are bound to find a way in. Again the higher the bed is from the ground the easier control will be.

The base of the bed should contain crocks or rubble to facilitate drainage. This should be covered with rough peat, straw or plastic drainage sheeting to prevent compost clogging up the drainage material.

There are two ways of preparing the bed for use depending on how you intend to grow your bulbs. The first is to fill the bed directly with compost in which the bulbs will grow and the second is to fill the bed with sand in which the pots containing bulbs will be plunged.

The compost is the same mixture that has been advocated throughout the book: John Innes No. 3 with an equal amount of extra grit (see p. 37). Variations on this will doubtless be made as the grower gains in experience and comes to prefer one mixture in favour of another in different circumstances. It should be well firmed down into the frame and the top 2.5cm (1in) or more should be covered with gravel.

The bulbs can be planted directly into the bed or within lattice pots. Bulbs have a terrible habit of wandering about, so if they are put in neat clumps throughout the frame, within two years they will be all over the place and it will be impossible to tell which bulb is which except when they are in flower. The bed should be divided up into compartments using aluminium sheeting or slates. Wood can be used but it naturally has the tendency to rot. Each compartment is then used for one type of bulb.

The other method is to use lattice pots. These were developed for the pond trade. Compost and plants are put in the container and then the whole thing is submerged into the pond, allowing the water in and the roots to wander free across the plastic liners. Alpine gardeners soon realised that they could be used for their own purposes. The bulbs were able to wander and multiply within the pot, but their roots could pass freely through the lattice looking for moisture and nourishment. When it was time to dig up the bulbs and split them the whole container could be lifted, leaving no little bulbs in the soil: an easier and more efficient job. Another advantage is that the label can be tied to the lattice so there is little chance of the bulbs becoming confused.

The other method is to grow the bulbs in clay or plastic pots in the conventional manner and to plunge them in sand. This is a particularly useful way of growing them if you want to display them at shows.

It is difficult to give a strict regime to follow when growing bulbs as their requirements are different and books on bulbs should be consulted as to when watering should start. Obviously the autumn flowering crocuses will need to be started into growth earlier than the spring flowering ones, but only experience and acquired knowledge will tell you which are which. It is normal to open the frames to allow the rain to penetrate during the late autumn and early winter. These are kept open as long as there is not excessive rain. It is also best to shut them down if it snows or the temperature threatens to go too far below freezing.

The bulbs should be kept moist while they are in growth but after they have died down water should be withheld until it is time for them to start in growth. Until recently it has been felt that bulbs should be kept bone dry during the dormant season, but now some people prefer to supply just the merest modicum of water at

1. *Narcissus clusii* grown in an alpine house

2. *Cyclamen graecum* which needs the protection
of an alpine house or bulb frame

3. *Ramonda myconi* growing in
a shady rock crevice

4. White and purple *Fritillaria meleagris* growing in a moist spot

5. *Adonis vernalis* in a scree bed

6. A bright form of *Aubrieta deltoidea* growing in a wall

7. A newly planted stone trough

8. A strong-coloured *Primula auricula*
growing in a scree bed

9. Spring in a Czechoslovakian rock garden

10. *Gypsophila cerastioides* flowering in the rock garden

11. The South African dwarf shrub *Euryops acraeus* needs a well-drained spot

12. *Genista lydia* well-suited on the top of a retaining wall

13. A well-furnished scree-bed

14. *Phlox* 'Olga' and a sempervivum on a rocky outcrop

15. The bulbous *Ipheion uniflorum* needs a sunny well-drained spot

16. *Rhodiola rosea* is a succulent that does well in the rock garden

17. *Crocus minimus* is a trouble-free bulb for the rock garden or bulb frame

18. A well-constructed rock garden

19. *Dianthus* 'Spark' is a very old cultivar

20. A colourful display of dwarf phlox spilling over a rock

16. *Rhodiola rosea* is a succulent that does well in the rock garden

17. *Crocus minimus* is a trouble-free bulb for the rock garden or bulb frame

18. A well-constructed rock garden

19. *Dianthus* 'Spark' is a very old cultivar

20. A colourful display of dwarf phlox spilling over a rock

the roots. Certainly plants such as *Cyclamen graecum* have responded very well to such treatment. Bulbs plunged in pots can have the plunge material kept just slightly moist. It is more difficult in a directly planted frame, but a small quantity of water poured into empty plastic pots sunk at the edge of the frame will spread underneath giving just the right amount of moisture.

Because of the free-draining nature of the compost, nutrients will be leached away. A light bonemeal or general feed should be given in winter as the bulbs come into growth and a potash liquid feed should be applied every two weeks while the plants are in growth. Bulbs in pots are usually repotted every year, during which time the compost is replaced thus almost eliminating the need to feed. Liquid feeds can be applied as for directly planted bulbs, but avoid making them over-lush otherwise they will be prone to disease.

In a bed the bulbs can be left in position for several years without their exhausting the compost. They should be lifted every three years or so and many clumps divided. One of the wonderful things about many bulbs is that they multiply themselves without any help from the grower, giving a constant supply of new bulbs to sell or give away.

Bulbs that do not require such a stringent summer drying can be grown in the open garden. Some prefer to have a warm sunny place up against a south-facing wall, which will probably be quite dry anyway. If no bulb frame nor alpine house is available, it is always possible to cover the bulbs in the open garden with a pane of glass during the summer.

Peat Beds

Now we come on to something completely different. If you think that alpine gardening is just about growing the cushion plants from the high altitudes, then this chapter is not for you. On the other hand if you also enjoy the many delights that flower farther down the mountainside then you should try and include a peat bed somewhere in your garden. There are so many exciting plants to grow, particularly from woodland areas, that I am surprised that more people do not create this type of bed. At the same time I am surprised that it is the alpine gardeners that have taken this type of gardening under their wing, because so many of the plants are herbaceous and bigger than the normal run of alpines. But in other ways I am not, because it seems to me the alpine gardeners have an eye for a good plant wherever it might grow. On the whole they are not so interested in the overall effect of the plants; they are more interested in the plants themselves. They are happy to grow plants from the Arctic down to the hot deserts and mountains of Iran.

All the continents, with the natural exception of Antarctica, produce woodland plants of note, many of which are given in the A–Z of Plants in Chapter 6. They consist of bulbous material as well as herbaceous and non-herbaceous perennials. The one thing they all have in common is their love of the deep, cool, nutritious leaf-mould on the floor of the woods and forests. Another common feature is that many of them grow in the deciduous woodlands, so that they flower early in the year before the leaf canopy is developed above their heads, shutting off the sun for the rest of the year. Others that flower later do so in dappled shade on the edge of the woodlands or in woodland glades. This shade and the leafy soil structure is what we aim for when we build our peat beds.

Siting

One of the good things about a peat bed is that it can go into space that has been left as unsuitable for other alpine features. It is possible to build it in the shade of the north side of a house or under trees, although to grow the biggest range of plants it is not desirable to have too dense a shade. If it is on the north side of a wall it is denied sunshine for most of the day but it still gets plenty of overhead light. The amount of light available under the trees varies. It is best to avoid conifers and deciduous trees with a dense canopy such as beech or horse chestnut. However, it is possible to build a bed on the north side of these so that they provide an indirect shade. Another problem with some trees, and again the horse chestnut is a good example, is that they are terribly hungry for both nutrients and moisture, and their roots will soon invade a rich bed. Trees with their branches cut high, letting in plenty of light but only dappled sunlight when the sun is at its fiercest and directly overhead are the best for shading a peat bed.

It is possible to build a peat bed in full sun and then cover it with a canopy of plastic greenhouse shading, supported on a metal or wooden framework. This does not look particularly elegant but that is of little consequence to the plants. The frame should be high enough to allow free access beneath it without bending. Only the top need be covered as it is the overhead sun that is the one that is to be kept out. The lower morning and evening suns that will slant in through the sides of the framework will cause little harm.

Not all plants that enjoy moisture and a cool root-run are shade-lovers. There are many that enjoy some sun, so it is a good idea to construct the bed, if you possibly can, with one area of it out in the sunshine for at least part of the day. Even many of the woodlanders will grow in sun as long as they are never allowed to dry out at the root, so if you are restricted to a sunny site it does not mean you should give up the idea of a peat bed.

It is possible to build a peat bed on chalky soil to accommodate ericaceous plants. It often occurs in nature that rhododendrons are found growing in pockets of peaty detritus on limestone mountains. The bed must be built above the soil level to prevent any lime leaching into the compost. The base can be covered with polythene but it must have drainage holes which will allow water out (and preferably not allow in the lime-laden water). These beds will often work for years when suddenly the ericaceous plants go chlorotic and die as lime manages to get in. It is a gamble, but if you do not want to risk the expense of the plants there are so many others that will tolerate lime that you will never be short of interesting and delightful plants.

Construction

The construction of a peat bed is very easy and should not cause too much of a problem. In spite of the plants' love of moisture, they do not like waterlogged conditions, so the first detail to attend to, as in all aspects of alpine gardening, is the drainage. Make certain the site is free from stagnant water. The bed can be built above ground, but if it is intended to have a sunken bed, any water that could accumulate beneath it should be drained away, possibly to a soakaway pit.

It is normal to make a raised peat bed above ground level. This allows plants to be displayed with more interest, including those growing in the vertical walls as well as on different levels. It also allows varying depths of soil, so that the deeper rooted plants can be planted on the higher, thus deeper, levels.

A peat bed constructed with peat block retaining walls

These raised beds will obviously need some supports, but if these are not available then it is perfectly feasible to have the beds at ground level without any variation in heights.

The supports used for general raised beds can also be used for the peat bed, namely stone, brick or concrete blocks, but wood and peat blocks are the best materials if you can get them. Wood can be in the form of thick planks of wood or railway sleepers, or it can be something less formal such as logs. These can be laid on their side, possibly two or three on top of one another if they are not very thick, or they can be cut and driven into the earth in a vertical position, a bit like a low level palisade.

The wood will ultimately rot, but this does not matter too much as, after all, we are trying to recreate woodland conditions, and rotting wood is part of that ecology. By the time it does rot, the roots of the plants will probably have bound the whole lot together, so that the soil will be held in its various levels in spite of the decay of its supports.

The other popular support for peat beds are peat blocks. These are, fortunately, becoming easier to find again, from specialist nurseries and even garden centres. They are laid like ordinary bricks and blocks with one layer overlapping the previous. Every so often it is a good idea to lay one block so that it goes back into the bed to tie in the wall. Again, once the bed is established roots will bind the whole thing together as a stable unit. Before peat blocks are laid they must be soaked in water, not sprinkled with a watering can but left soaking in water for at least a day. This means it needs a bit of forethought before you start building.

The filling of the bed depends somewhat on your own personal taste and the availability of materials. In spite of its name it is not constructed completely of peat. A good mixture would be one part loam, one part peat, one part leaf-mould and one part grit. Grit turns up even in a mixture for moisture lovers in which it has two functions, both of which sound contradictory. In the first place it is there to prevent excess moisture hanging around, i.e. improving the drainage, and in the second it is there to help the bed absorb moisture. If peat is allowed to dry out it is the devil to remoisten, the water will run off the surface. The presence of grit allows the water to penetrate into the bed and consequently allows the peat to become wet again.

The mixture can be varied at will. If you have a good friable soil, possibly already containing leaf-mould if it is near trees, then the addition of peat may be sufficient. The important thing is that the soil should retain moisture without becoming waterlogged.

Like all the other types of bed it is worth topdressing the peat bed, but instead of gravel, chipped bark makes an ideal covering. It conserves moisture and helps to keep down weeds. It will also help to keep out frosts as it has quite an insulating quality.

The beds will undoubtedly sink as they settle leaving the walls higher than the content. They will need topping up after a while with the same compost.

Many peat beds are constructed in such a manner that it is impossible to reach all parts of it from the surrounding path. Although the bed should be firmed before planting, constant walking on it will compact it too much. It is essential, therefore, to place some slabs of stone on the bed to form sufficient stepping and standing stones to allow access for weeding and for looking at the plants.

Planting can be carried out when the bed is complete or while it is in the process of construction. The latter particularly refers to the insertion of plants into the peat walls as they are built up. The vertical walls are ideal places for planting *Ramonda, Primula* and many other such plants: their roots will help to bind the bed together.

Maintenance

This is quite easy. The most important thing is to make certain that the bed does not dry out. This is particularly important with any peat blocks that have been used as walls. If these dry out they will shrink, leaving a gap between them and the compost in the bed. Not only will they be extremely difficult to re-wet but they are liable to collapse and, worse still, any plants that are growing through the blocks will have their roots exposed where they enter the bed. It is possible to install a permanent sprinkler system, or even an underground system, but these are expensive and an ordinary garden sprinkler will supply enough water.

A light feed of a general fertiliser can be applied in the late winter and it can be topdressed with extra peat or a new covering of chipped bark.

Weeds can be a problem in peat beds as the moisture is ideal for their growth. It is best regularly to remove any that are seen, rather than to leave it and then have a 'blitz', as the latter is rarely satisfactory. One problem when weeding peat beds is that when a weed is pulled up a lot of peat adheres to the roots, so that wihout care much of the peat can be removed from the bed. The mulch of chipped bark not only helps to keep the weeds down, but is not so susceptible to being removed in this way.

Water in the rock garden

Water is a natural feature that occurs in the mountains, many plants growing at its margins or even in it. In the rock garden, water is, as much as anything, a decorative feature. Many of the plants that can be grown near water can be grown in a peat bed, so the lack of a pool or stream does not necessarily inhibit the number of plants that can be grown. The pool does provide an alternative habitat though and one that can look extremely attractive if attention has been given to its construction.

Lucky is he who has natural water running through his garden. The largest private rock garden I have seen (5,000 sq m, 1¼ acres), had three natural streams passing through it. Under normal circumstances they were placid, providing a constant level throughout the year, but every few years there would be a severe storm and half the rock garden would be washed away. This is told as a cautionary tale, because although natural water is the ideal in many respects it can also have an uncontrollable destructive force. If a stream is used there should be a bypass for any surge.

For most people the water in any rock garden is an artificial feature, with water being circulated by a pump. It is possible to have just a pool but it is better, both visually and from the plants' point of view, if the water can be moving. The water in the mountains is constantly on the move, its tumbling bubbling movement constantly re-oxygenating it. In the rock garden the design is usually with a pool at the top of the outcrop, with a small stream tumbling down through a channel to a lower pool from whence it is pumped back to the top. Small bog gardens can be created in the marginal pockets and plants set into rock crevices overlooking the water where they are kept cool and receive sufficient moisture.

Design and construction of a water feature gives plenty of scope to the imagination: the variations that can be dreamt up are almost infinite. Unfortunately, though, the materials used dictate that once in place the pools and stream bed cannot be easily remade without starting again. Because the beds are falling over a distance and perhaps twisting at the same time, ponds and streams are very difficult to construct out of pond-liner or polythene. The best material is concrete. This is easier to shape and, perhaps more to the point, easier to disguise with rocks and vegetation.

There are several good books on constructing pools and streams, which go into the mechanics in detail. If you are thinking of constructing an elaborate scheme then it might be a good idea to buy or borrow one of these. Here, I will briefly outline the basic construction details of the two aspects of a water garden: above and below ground.

Below ground are the mechanics for moving the water from the bottom pool to the top of the system. The simplest system is to have a submersible pump in the bottom pool which constantly pushes the water uphill into the top via a plastic pipe. The water at the top can emerge as a hidden spring trickling into the pool or directly into the pool, giving it a constant ripple. Alternatively the water can be drawn off through a pipe to a pump chamber, where the pump is hidden in a dry hole beneath a slab or rock and thence to the top. Follow the installation instructions supplied with the pump very carefully as water and electricity are a very dangerous combination. If in any doubt at all consult a qualified engineer.

In both these schemes the water level in the system is kept topped up manually by pouring water into one of the pools. A more sophisticated system includes a cistern below ground in which a ball float will automatically open a valve if the water level drops, allowing more water to enter direct from the main water system.

Above ground the instructions are not quite so simple as much will depend on the design and on the structure of the existing rock garden. If possible it is best to install it while the rock garden as a whole is being built. However bad you are at drawing, try and sketch out what you hope to achieve, both in a plan (i.e. looking down on the garden) and in cross section.

Excavate the pools and the bed of the stream: the holes should be much larger than the intended size. This should not be a problem if your ground naturally slopes but if you are constructing a rock garden on the flat, then subsidence can cause problems in the future. Soil should be rammed in as hard as possible beneath the structure and preferably left for a while to settle. The beds are then lined with rubble. This is covered with a 7.5cm (3in) layer of concrete, more if there is a chance of subsidence. Make the mix on the dryish side so that it can be shaped around the edges of the pool; too wet a mix will slide to the bottom of the pool leaving weak sides. When dry the whole is given a surface layer of cement (one part cement, three parts builders' sand).

Stones can be incorporated in the design at the wet concrete stage but they should not go right through the concrete otherwise a leak will soon develop. An obvious position for stones is as lips from which the water can either drip or pour from one level to another. The edges of the pool and stream should be disguised with rocks so that as little of the cement shows as possible. Any that does will look very raw at first but will soon tone down and blend with the rest of the structure.

The whole thing should be as watertight as possible, with water being contained within the pools and stream. Any loss through cracks or over the edge will have to be made up. Topping up will be necessary from time to time because of evaporation.

The piping for the pump can go through the bottom or side of the lower pool but this will cause a weak spot and it is better to arrange for the pipe to leave the pool over the edge, hidden from view by a rock. An overflow pipe can also be disguised in this manner. This pipe can take water right away, possibly to a rubble-filled soakaway, or can supply a damp bed of some kind, for example a peat bed.

Some gardeners do not like watering their plants with water drawn directly from the tap because of the additives, such as chlorine, used to clean it up. In the water garden the problems are lessened because once the water enters the system it is aerated by falling down from one pool to another and any toxic gases will quickly evaporate. There is a problem with hard water which will contain lime. If you are unfortunate to draw your water from a hard water area (and this is not the same as living in a limestone or chalk area — your water may come from some way away) then you may not be able to grow any calcifuges (lime-haters) in the vicinity of the water garden.

Small bog gardens can be created in shallow dishes on the margins of either the pool or the stream. Other plants will relish being planted in overhanging rock crevices. A wide range of plants can be used, but there can be a temptation to use plants that are too large for a rock garden; the scale of the surroundings must be borne in mind when making a selection. It is possible that the bottom pool is outside the main rock garden and much larger than one constructed within it. Here it may be feasible to grow some of the larger plants such as hostas and lysichiton. Lists of the appropriate plants appear in Appendix I.

The question of fish I leave to you.

Other situations

Being small, alpines have the advantage of not taking up much space, but, in spite of this, space always seems to be at a premium in the garden. There are a surprising number of odd spaces around the garden that can be adapted for growing alpines, increasing the scope and number of plants grown. If you look around the garden with an imaginative eye, I am sure you will see some of these areas. This section is written to give you a few ideas of the type of space that can be utilised.

Porches

Many porches have low tile roofs and these make ideal places to create small gardens of plants that do not mind being dried out occasionally. On my own porch roof is a wonderful garden of sedum and sempervivum mixed in with moss and lichen.

In Britain, these were often created in country areas and the traditional way of starting them is to put a cow pat on the roof and put the sempervivum or sedum into it. Not the normal procedure for alpine gardeners, but a very effective one! The colony of plants soon build up trapping dust and other detritus forming a small rock garden. Apart from the initial planting no attention is ever needed.

The one on my porch has been there for very many years and does not seem to do any damage to the tiles or roof, but is a great source of comment, particularly when it is alight with the blaze of bright yellow from the *Sedum acre*. It is on the north side of the cottage and gets protection from the full sun. I am not certain whether the south side of a building might be too hot and dry, but such plants grow happily in walls of this aspect.

This idea can be used on any low building, such as a garage or a shed. The plants look best against tiles, but doubtless other materials will do.

Gravel areas

There are various types of material that can be used either as paths, drives or on terraces. Gravel is one of the traditional materials that is still very popular. As well as having a warm colour and a soft edge it has a welcoming crunch when trodden. It is normal to keep these areas weed-free, usually with chemical herbicides, but if there is a reasonable depth of gravel and you do not mind plants growing in it, gravel makes an ideal scree bed.

One can grow the tougher plants in there, such as the thymes which do not mind being knocked about a bit. Other plants can be annuals or short-lived perennials that seed themselves around, such as *Erinus alpinus*.

Drives

Many driveways consist of two rows of solid concrete or paving stones, for the wheels to go on, and an empty strip between, often put down to grass or just left to grow weeds. This makes an ideal position to try out an alpine lawn. Clear the area of perennial weeds, lighten the soil and then plant some of the carpeters such as thyme and the other plants suggested in Appendix I under alpine lawns.

The other possibility is to use the area for some of the rampant plants, such as the pratias that you would not dare use near a rock bed. The concrete runways of the drive will act as a barrier, preventing the plants from getting into the rest of the garden.

Window boxes

It is quite possible to grow alpines in window boxes. Basically the techniques are the same as for troughs, but two important aspects must be stressed. The first is that any container attached to a window sill above the ground is potentially very dangerous. Make certain that it is well secured. If in doubt about your ability to install it, get a professional to do it. The second point is that window boxes, exposed to the winds and sun, are liable to dry out very rapidly, so water every day if necessary.

Virtually all the plants that can be grown in troughs will grow in a window box. Those that are on the fragile side should be avoided as these can be blown to pieces in an exposed position.

Other containers

Many other containers besides sinks and troughs can be used to house alpines, chimney pots and plastic containers being alternatives that are frequently seen. There is no limit to what can be used but please do remember the dignity of the plant. The plant will not mind where it grows as long as it has the right conditions, but there are some situations that obviously look wrong. Plastic and alpines never seem to mix very happily visually (except for flower pots and even here the relationship is not too happy). Try not to use alpines as brash containerised bedding plants, their simplicity and beauty would be in jeopardy.

Shady areas

Shade has been mentioned throughout the book in different locations throughout the garden (including the north-facing porch above) but perhaps a few general words should be said about it.

If your garden is in the shade for a large part or all of the day, then there are still a lot of alpine plants that you can grow. It is important to choose parts of the garden that have plenty of light although they have no direct sunlight. Overhanging trees should be avoided, for example.

A peat garden is one possibility, where many of the plants are woodlanders and are used to shade. Apart from these there are many of the higher alpines which will tolerate some shade; saxifrages for example. It is more difficult to find plants that will tolerate dry shade, particularly that found under trees. *Cyclamen hederifolium* is one species that will live in such a place, and some of the euphorbias and sedum will also grow there. The range of plants will increase if leaf-mould and peat are added to the soil so that it holds moisture. Anemones, arums and bulbs such as snowdrops and trilliums can be grown, along with a host of other plants that are advocated for the peat garden.

Like so many things in alpine gardening, imagination and determination to learn will soon provide the answers to problem areas such as shade.

5 Techniques

There is much more to alpine gardening than buying plants and sticking them in a bed; they must be looked after and increased. Some people think that this is a chore, particularly activities like weeding and tidying up, but approached with the right frame of mind, even these can be a delight. It gives one a chance to examine the plants closely; at all stages of their growth, not just when in flower.

Propagation

To many gardeners the height of gardening is propagation: the skill to produce new plants from what appears to be a speck of dust or a slip of vegetation. To others it is just a means to an end: a way of providing more plants. Whatever one's attitude, propagation is a skill worth acquiring for many reasons:

— To multiply one's own plants to provide extra stock for the garden and to give away.
— To grow plants that are not available in commerce.
— To be able to grow plants from seed obtained from seed exchanges or collecting expeditions.
— To safeguard the loss of rare or precious plants in one's garden.
— To safeguard plants in the wild; it is preferable to propagate wild plants rather than dig them up.
— For the sheer joy of it.

Seed

Seed is the commonest way of propagating plants. If you are used to growing seed from commercial outlets then you will be familiar with the routine, but only partly. Commercial seed is selected to provide a quick and a near 100 per cent germination; otherwise customers complain. Much of this seed comes from Mediterranean annuals which have a tendency to germinate all at the same time. Alpine plants tend to hedge their bets and put up certain barriers so that they will not germinate unless the conditions are right and even then they do not all germinate at once, but possibly over several seasons. This is a safeguard mechanism to ensure the species' survival.

Not all beginners realise that alpine seed can be different from that of commercial bedding plants and believe they have failed if they do not get total germination within a fortnight of sowing. It is much more difficult to produce plants from alpine seed (or other non-commercial seed for that matter); undoubtedly some will grow like the proverbial mustard and cress, but others will be a total failure. Do not despair if you do get a total failure, keep on trying and experimenting; that is what alpine gardening is all about.

Although sowing from seed is the commonest method of reproducing plants it is not the most accurate. Seed not only takes the characteristics of the parent on which it is produced, but is also likely to contain elements of its pollen parent and its forebears. Thus a blue-flowered plant may produce a different shade of blue, or white or pink flowers. The plant may not even be the same species; it could be a hybrid between its two parents if cross pollination has taken place. This is bad news if you want identical plants but good news if you want the opportunity of looking for good variations on the original plant. Some plants interbreed very easily and itinerant bees provide the means for this to be accomplished. If you want a species to remain pure, and you know it can be promiscuous, then you will need to isolate it from others. On the other hand if you deliberately want to make the cross, then hand pollinate the plants using a soft brush, making certain that no insect can come behind you and repeat your work with pollen of another plant (i.e. cover the pollinated head with a muslin bag or keep it in a closed frame until the flower fades).

The safest method of reproducing identical plants is by cuttings or division, which are dealt with later.

Composts

First we will look at sowing composts and then move on to the methods of dealing with the seed. Seed compost is a medium in which the seed starts its life as a growing plant. The only thing that it requires of the medium is moisture; seed has its own built-in store of food. This is why seed can be started into growth on damp tissue paper. As the seed grows it requires somewhere for its searching roots to find moisture and nutrients and to give it physical support, i.e. to stop it falling over. If the seedlings are pricked out at an early stage in their growth then the amount of nutrients they need in the soil is small as they will have got thus far on their own reserves from within the seed. However, if the seedlings are left in the sowing compost for any length of time after germination, then they will need some form of nutrients on which to grow and develop.

What this amounts to in practical terms is that if you prick out your plants at an early stage then the precise formula of the sowing compost is unimportant, you can use almost anything (one famous grower always uses spent potting compost), as long as it will contain moisture and is free from disease. For the majority of growers there is no guaranteeing as to when the plants will be pricked out and it is safer to use a formulated compost in which there are nutrients that are available to give the plant a good start in life.

As with all composts there are two basic choices between a soil-based compost and a soilless compost. The choice is often up to the grower's personal preference, rather than the plant's; many growers defend their choice as the correct one. Some seed do better in the peat-based composts, particularly the ericaceous plants but they will also grow in soil-based composts as long as there is no lime present. There are two problems that can occur with the soilless composts. Some plants find it difficult to adjust when moved from such a compost into the normal growing medium which is soil-based. The other problem is that the soilless compost must under no circumstances be allowed to dry out; if it does it is virtually impossible to re-wet, and anyway, by then the plants will be dead. Experiment and see which is most satisfactory for your style of gardening.

Both composts can be purchased from nurseries and garden centres. The former is likely to be based on a John Innes Seed Compost formula which consists of:

2 parts sterilised loam
1 part moss peat or leaf-mould
1 part sharp sand

To each 36 litres (8gal) is added:

42g (1½oz) superphosphate
21g (¾oz) ground limestone

Use a special ericaceous mix which omits the limestone for lime-hating plants. Since it is normal for pots to be stood in the open until germination occurs, sometimes two or more years, they are subjected to rainfall, which can be heavy at times, so it is advisable to provide for extra drainage by adding at least one extra part of grit or sharp sand to the above formula. The same is true for the soilless composts where the peat will become saturated and stagnant unless extra drainage is given.

The loam and leaf-mould, if used, should be sterilised to eliminate any weed seedlings or pests that might relish fresh seedlings.

Sources of seed

The most obvious source of seed is to buy it from a commercial seed merchant. This is the normal channel through which most people buy seed before they get involved with growing alpines. It does not take long to realise the general seed merchants have very few alpines on their lists.

Anyone growing alpines should join the Alpine Garden Society. This provides a wealth of information and contact with other growers. Of immediate concern, they run a Seed Exchange in which nearly 5,000 different species and varieties are offered. There are other societies including the American Rock Garden Society which provide a similar service. Another advantage of joining a society is that you soon meet other like-minded people at local group meetings, shows and other events and this inevitably leads to exchanging plants and seed. One must not forget that seed can be collected from one's own plants, either for use or giving away (collecting will be dealt with later).

Later as experience grows there are plenty of seed collecting expeditions to remote mountain areas in which shares can be taken. The current price is usually £50 ($85), which may seem a lot, but the shareholder usually receives at least 50 packets for this and sometimes a 100 or more depending on the success of the expedition.

Receipt of seed

What to do with the seed when it arrives? Should it be sown or stored? Opinions differ on this, as with so many other aspects of alpine gardening. There are undoubtedly some genera such as the Primulaceae and the Ranunculaceae that benefit from sowing as fresh as possible. If you sow, for example, the pasque flower, *Pulsatilla vulgaris*, fresh from the plant you will get a high percentage of germination, leave it to the spring and the result can be dismal.

On the other hand if you sow everything while it is fresh, i.e. in the late summer and autumn, you will get a fair amount of immediate germination and then you will have the problem of getting the seedlings through the winter.

One of the reasons why seed needs an early sowing is so that it can experience the winter frosts which will break its natural dormancy. In the wild alpine seed could germinate as soon as it falls to the ground, but it would then have to face the severe winter conditions to which it would probably succumb. To counter this the seed has a built-in mechanism which needs a series of frosts or cold weather followed by warmer conditions that tell it that it has passed through winter and it is now safe to germinate.

Those that need to be freshly sown, such as the Ranunculaceae (*Ranunculus, Helleborus, Anemone, Pulsatilla, Hepatica, Aquilega, Eranthis, Delphinium* and many others) should be sown as soon as possible. Others should be sown early in the year, say January and left out in the frosts; this will break the dormancy of any that require such treatment. The other way to break this type of dormancy is to keep the seed in a refrigerator for a few weeks. This is an ideal way of storing seed anyway. Put the seed into a sealed plastic box as soon as you receive it and put it in the refrigerator. This will help to prolong the seed's viability, even those that normally need sowing fresh, and at the same time give those that need it a chilling to break dormancy.

Sowing

Most people prefer to use plastic pots for sowing seed. The compost must be kept moist all the time and there is less chance of plastic pots drying out. With bedding plants it is quite normal to sow a whole trayful; with alpines it is only necessary to sow 7.5cm (3in) pots. These will provide more than enough plants for most uses. If there is a large amount of seed, then either several pots or larger ones can be used. Trays are rarely used as they are very shallow and dry out far too quickly.

The sowing compost is put in the pots and then firmed down. The seed is sown thinly on the top and then covered with a layer of grit. For some curious reason, all the books one reads on gardening tell you to sieve the compost over the seeds to cover them with a depth equal to half the depth of the seed. In spite of this oft-repeated advice, nearly all alpine growers cover their seed not with sieved soil, but lumps of grit, and not in a thin layer but up to 2cm (¾in) thick. This harsh treatment obviously works otherwise no one would do it. The conventional method has been handed down from past practices and has little to recommend it.

The advantages of the grit covering are several: to reiterate — sieved compost pans down into a hard layer very quickly after the first watering. Subsequent watering runs off the top of this pan and down the sides of the compost, leaving that in the middle unwetted. Fine compost and seeds can be washed to one side of the pot if it is uneven; grit holds everything in place, preventing panning and allowing even penetration. Grit acts as a free-draining, dry collar around the neck of the plant which is very prone to rotting if left in contact with overwet compost. The pot does not dry out too rapidly as the grit acts as a mulch. It also acts as a mulch by helping to keep down weeds, mosses and liverwort that can form in damp pots. If they do form it is easy to remove the grit, along with the interloper and replace it with fresh grit. It is much more difficult to remove the top layer of compost without damaging the seedlings.

These are just a few of the advantages that alpine gardeners have found in using a grit topping to their seed pots. The size of grit used is that which is known as chick grit or poultry grit and is available, by the sack, from agricultural merchants, or sometimes in smaller quantities from pet stores.

Once the dressing is in place the pot can be watered, either from beneath by standing it in a tray of water or from above with a watering can. The pot should then be placed outside in a shady place, to take anything the weather throws at it. If the amount of drainage material in the compost is adequate it will be able to stand any amount of rain, but if there is any doubt, the pots should be covered during prolonged periods of rainfall. The pots should be kept out of direct sunlight, possibly up against a north wall or hedge.

There is generally no need to provide warmth for germinating alpine seed. The natural increase in temperature at the end of winter will be enough to break dormancy. It is only those plants that come from tropical and the hotter regions (which includes most of the bedding plants) that need extra warmth and the use of propagators. Some growers, however, do use a little bottom heat to speed up germination.

One very important aspect must not be overlooked: labelling. This should be done immediately as one pot of seed looks very much like another and a few seconds after sowing it is possible to forget what is in which pot. The label should contain the name of the plant, the date of sowing and the source. If the seed has a collector's number this should be included. If there are only a few seeds in the pot, say up to six, then the exact number should be recorded. This helps you to know when no more can be expected to germinate. Some people like to keep a sowing register in book form, which contains the information already mentioned plus future information such as when the seed germinated, when it was pricked out, and so on.

Pricking out

An eye should be kept on the pots to look out for those which have germinated. Some people transfer those pots that have germinated to the alpine house, others keep them outside in a cold frame. In either case they should not be allowed to dry out nor be exposed to strong sunlight. With the majority of plants, they are ready for pricking out as soon as the first two true leaves are formed. The first leaves are the seed leaves and are usually quite different from the adult leaves, the next pair are the true leaves and when these have developed it is time to prick out. This involves transplanting the seedling into individual pots of potting compost.

The seedling should be carefully handled by the seed leaves. Most plants can be pricked out into 7.5cm (3in) pots, but vigorous growers may want to go straight into 9cm (3½in) pots. If you are short of space or pots it is sometimes possible to use a larger pot and put several seedlings in it. If you use trays, make certain they are deep ones. The normal plastic ones sold in garden centres are too shallow for most purposes. Once transplanted a topdressing of grit is applied and the pot watered from below by standing it in a water bath.

Freshly transplanted seedlings, or any repotted plant for that matter, should be kept out of direct sunlight in a closed frame for a few days before it is hardened off (gradually opening the frame for longer each day). It can then be placed in an open frame.

Sometimes a pot of seed will germinate over one or two years. If one seedling comes up and it looks as if there is going to be no more that year, it is possible carefully to remove it, refill the hole with compost and leave until more germinate.

Bulbs should be left in the same pot until after they have died down after their second year. They can then be knocked out of the pot and planted singly or in groups in fresh compost. Some growers advocate trying to keep the bulbs in growth for as long as possible and transplanting in the second year by repotting the whole rootball, without disturbing the soil, into a larger pot. Keeping seedling bulbs in the same compost means they will want the occasional liquid feed.

Collecting seed

It is a good practice to collect seed from the plants in your own garden. You will be able to use it for propagating more plants, giving to friends or offering to seed exchanges. It will also give you experience in collecting seed which will be invaluable should you have the opportunity of obtaining it from the wild. Another advantage of collecting seed is that it gives you the opportunity to look at the plants after they have finished flowering. Many people miss this stage and never see the many curious receptacles that nature has devised for carrying seed.

The main problem is working out when the seed is ripe for collecting. Some is ready in a remarkably short time after the flower dies, others such as cyclamen take six months or more. Experience and vigilance will tell you when to collect. Normally the seeds change colour on ripening from green to black, brown, orange or red. Similarly the seed pods change from a fleshy to a sere or brittle container, ready to split and shed its seed. Again this is accompanied by a colour change. Some seed indicates that it is ripe by its readiness to leave the plant. The seed of buttercups will be readily rubbed off by the fingers when ripe and the pappus of a composite will come away very easily as soon as it is ready to blow off in the wind.

Some plants, such as the tulips and fritillaries, hold up chalices of seed waiting to be picked, others, such as hellebores suddenly split, while apparently still green, depositing the whole lot of seed directly on to the ground. Others, such as the geraniums, have an explosive mechanism that throws the seed vast distances: these are the most difficult to harvest; timing is most crucial. If there is the opportunity to visit the plants daily, experience will soon teach the gardener when is the best time to collect the seed. He will begin to recognise by the change in colour when a geranium capsule is about to explode and to harvest it before it has a chance to do so.

If the whole seed head ripens at once then the whole head can be cut off and put directly into a paper bag. Remember to label the bag immediately. Remove capsules individually if they ripen at differing times and again put into a bag. With smaller, cushion plants, it will be necessary to get down on your knees and patiently remove the seed individually with a pair of tweezers. If you have missed the point of ripening, it may still be possible to pick up the shed seed from within the cushion using the same tweezer technique. Explosive seed can be picked just as it ripens as explained above or muslin bags can be attached to catch the flying seed.

Storage initially should be in paper bags. These should be left open, unless they contain explosive seed heads. This will help them to dry off, which is very important. Never use polythene bags at this stage as they cause the seed to rot. Store the bags in a cool, airy place that is not in direct sunlight.

When dry the seed should be cleaned and all chaff and debris removed. This can be done with the fingers or by gently blowing over the seed. Fine dust can be removed by putting the seed into a fine sieve when the seed and larger debris will stay behind. This larger debris can then be removed by putting it into a coarser sieve where the seed passes through.

When the seed is dry and clean it can be stored in either plastic or paper packets. It should be kept in a cool dry place or in a refrigerator as described at the beginning of this chapter. At all stages it is important to remember to label the packets.

Cuttings

Cuttings is one of the four methods of vegetative propagation (the others being division, layering and grafting). Vegetative methods of propagation are important as not all plants can be reproduced from seed. Some do not set seed, or at least not in cultivation, and others, while producing seed, do not produce offspring identical to their parent. The latter consideration is quite important as it is often desirable to produce plants that resemble each other in every way. For example, named forms of plants have normally been isolated and named from the rest of the species because they carry some desirable characteristics; they may have larger flowers, be more vigorous, more hardy or of a better colour. If such a plant is reproduced from seed there is no guarantee that all or any of these will appear in the new plants. On the other hand if the plants are reproduced vegetatively then all these character-istics will be carried over; it is possible to reproduce the same plant over and over again. A plant raised from seed cannot bear its parent's cultivar name even if it looks identical, a plant raised from a cutting, or by other vegetative means, may.

Another advantage of cuttings over seed is that a cutting will root and grow away into a mature plant much more quickly than a seed can. In some cases the seed may still be waiting to germinate when the cutting is already planted out in the rock garden.

Composts

Cuttings composts are very easy to make, so easy that they are hardly worth buying ready-made. Basically they are just a medium to support the plant physically and to provide it with moisture.

The mixture that most people use is a straightforward 50 per cent sharp sand and 50 per cent sieved peat. The peat is sometimes replaced with Perlite, which can be purchased at most garden centres. This has the property of holding moisture which it readily gives up to the roots of plants.

Propagators

Cuttings can be grown without any protection whatsoever (witness hardwood cuttings bedded directly into the open garden), but better results can be achieved if the atmosphere around the cutting is kept close to prevent too high a rate of transpiration. This is achieved, as we will see later, by reducing the amount of leaf area on the cutting, but also by enclosing the cutting either within solid walls or a wall of mist.

The simplest container is a polythene bag in which the pot bearing the cuttings is placed. A wire hoop may be used to prevent the cutting touching the polythene, which may cause it to rot. This is easy, cheap and generally works, but I have never been really happy with it as a method. One reason for this is that it is not easy to remove the condensation from the inside of the bag (although the bag can be turned inside out once a day). This makes it difficult to see the cuttings and it is quite a lot of trouble to take the bag off and replace it without its touching the cuttings.

I find it better to use a more rigid-sided propagator. The simplest of these are plastic jars or bottles with the neck cut off. These sit over the top of the cuttings pot, can be easily taken off and with a flick of the wrist any condensation can be removed. It is possible to have some with holes in the top to replace the closed ones during the weaning process.

A slightly larger version of this is the plastic propagators that one can buy from garden centres. These have vents at the top which can be opened to help with the hardening off process.

Moving up the scale, most growers who propagate a lot will want to have a propagating frame (see also p. 34). This is a very simple structure of four walls and a sloping roof of glass. For those built inside the alpine house the walls can be of wood (preferably painted white inside to provide maximum light for the cuttings) or aluminium. Both these materials can be used outside but the aluminium can be a bit cold during the winter. Brick or concrete blocks can also be used for frames built in the open.

The size of the frames depend on how many cuttings you are likely to produce. It is always better to have more than one frame then you can be using one to harden off rooted cuttings while the other is kept closed. They can be built on to the bench of the alpine house, or if there is plenty of light, under the bench. Some houses have them running the full length of the benching.

Cuttings can be put directly into the rooting medium that fills the floor of the frame or in pots which are stood or plunged within the frame. The depth of frames using the former method need not be as deep as those where the depth of the pot needs to be taken into consideration. The area covered by the frame does not matter too much; mine were determined by the size of the glass I had available when I constructed them.

A refinement that can be added is bottom heat. Here soil heating cables are laid in the bottom of the frame, in sand along with a thermostat to keep the temperature at the required level. Cables can also be placed around the inside of the frame to keep the air temperature constant, but most people find that the soil cables are sufficient. I have a set which I have been meaning to install for the last ten years, but I have found that I can root most things without the heat. However, there is no doubt that bottom heat does speed up the rooting process. The choice is yours.

A further refinement that is used in most commercial production of plants from cuttings is a mist unit. Here the cuttings are placed in pots on the open bench and are periodically sprayed with a fine mist. The spray system automatically comes on when a special metal 'leaf' dries out. This is a most effective method of growing cuttings, particularly when coupled with bottom heat. It is available to the amateur grower, but only worth it if you intend to produce a lot of plants. I would recommend growing cuttings in the traditional way first to gain experience and move on to the 'high tech' methods when this has been achieved.

Propagation units within the alpine house probably need no further protection, except in very cold areas where insulation material can be simply draped over these if necessary. Frames that are free-standing outside may need more protection. Some people make the walls double skinned and use some form of double glazing for the roof. This can take the form of two layers of glass in one light or two lights, one supported on an inner frame, i.e. a frame within a frame. Again on particularly cold nights these can be covered with insulation, an old carpet or hessian being the traditional materials.

Techniques

Cuttings are usually classified as to the ripeness of the material involved. Thus there are softwood, semi-ripe and hardwood cuttings. All three are applied in alpine gardening although the first two are the commonest.

Looking at softwood cuttings first, here the shoots are collected while the plant is

Taking cuttings

in growth, usually from late spring to late summer. The shoots to select are those that have no flowering buds on them; if this is impossible, and it is with some floriferous species, then it is still worth trying a shoot having first removed the flower buds. The second method uses semi-ripe material from the more woody species. Here the shoots are just beginning to harden and the plant is still in growth. This is usually in the summer. The same type of non-flowering shoots are collected. For most purposes with alpine plants it is preferable to try and take softwood cuttings.

The shoots must be moved from the plant to the cuttings frame as quickly as possible to prevent wilting. This can be aided by temporarily storing the material, as it is cut, in a polythene bag. Having arrived at your bench with a bag of cuttings, remove them one by one. Opinion over the length of the cutting varies, but with some species, for example, you are limited to short material anyway. Other material can vary from 2.5–7.5cm (1–3in).

Slice through the cutting with a scalpel or razor blade just below a node (where the leaf joins the stem). If the collected material was longer than you need then cut at the required length just above a leaf. More than one cutting can be made from a stem. The cutting taken from the top of the stem can include the tip of the shoot as long as this is not a flower bud.

One of the problems is to ensure that the cutting does not wilt. With a large leaf area, it will transpire at a faster rate than it can pick up water: remember at this stage it has no roots. The normal practice is reduce the transpirational area by removing most of the leaves, leaving just one pair at the top of the shoot. If a mist unit is used, then this is not so important as transpiration is reduced by saturating the air around the cutting with moisture. Enclosing the cuttings in a frame has the same effect, but to a lesser degree, necessitating the reduction of leaf area. However many leaves are removed it is essential to remove those that will be on the portion of the stem that goes below ground. If these remain, then rotting is likely to take place. The leaves should be removed cleanly with no pieces adhering to the stem that may rot.

The cutting should be put into the moist cutting compost as soon as possible. Before doing so it is advisable to dip the tip of the shoot that will go below ground in rooting hormone powder. Many of the plants will root quite happily without this treatment, but the powder usually contains a fungicide and this is useful in the prevention of rotting. In theory a hole should be made, the cutting inserted and the compost firmed around it. In practice many people just push the cutting into the compost. The reason for not taking the lazy route is to prevent damage to the cutting when it is pushed into the sharp sand. Also if hormone rooting powder has been used, it will get forced off as the cutting is inserted.

The cuttings should never be allowed to dry out, but on the other hand condensation on the lid should be wiped off to prevent its dripping on the plants. As much light as possible should be provided, but they should be kept out of direct sunlight. If in an alpine house, then the general house shading should be sufficient, but if it is in a separate frame then either paint or net shading will be necessary.

The cuttings are left in the propagator until they have rooted. It is not always possible to tell when this occurs. One of the indications is that the cutting starts to put on new growth. Another method is to pull the cutting gently and if resistance is met then there are roots holding it back. However, this method should be used sparingly because if the cutting is just putting out roots these can be severely damaged. It can be used where there are a large number of cuttings and the loss of one does not matter. Some cuttings will root very quickly, others can take a long time, particularly those taken later in the year. Some of these may take until the following spring before they put down roots.

When rooting has taken place, the propagator is gradually opened, allowing the plants to harden off. If the cuttings have been inserted in pots then the pot can be removed to a hardening off frame, leaving the other pots to continue rooting. If the cuttings are inserted directly into the compost in the base of the propagator then the whole lot will have to be hardened off at once.

When they have been fully hardened off the newly rooted plants are potted up into the appropriate sized pots using the normal potting compost. They should be left in a shaded, closed frame for a couple of days and then hardened off again.

Hardwood cuttings are a method of propagating trees and shrubs, occasionally used by the alpine gardener. Here, as the name implies, material is taken from mature wood after growth has stopped. These cuttings can be treated in the same way as above, overwintering the cuttings in the frame or they can be bedded down in the open garden in a sheltered site in the same way as roses are propagated.

There are two other types of cuttings that can be used: leaf and root cuttings. A few alpines can be grown from each of these methods. The former include some of the primulas, ramondas and sedums in particular. The leaves should be cut off as close to the main stem as possible, using a sharp knife. The base of the leaves are inserted just below the surface of the cutting compost and then treated in the same way as other cuttings.

All gardeners are familiar with root cuttings, although they might not think of it in that way. If the roots of dandelions are broken off while attempting to remove them and then left in the ground, they will shoot again. This is the basis of root cuttings. Fleshy roots are cut into sections of about 2.5–5cm (1–2in) and placed in cutting compost. It is essential to get the cuttings the right way up and it is usual to make a slanting cut on the lower part of the cutting and a straight cut at the top to help identify the direction of planting. *Morisia monanthos* is the classic example as a subject for this treatment, but there are several others including *Primula denticulata*.

Division

Many plants lend themselves to simple division. This means digging up the plant and splitting it into two or more pieces and either replanting directly back into the soil or into a pot. With wide-spreading plants, it is often possible to split off a rooted piece of the plant, with a trowel or spade, without disturbing the parent plant.

Some plants, like *Gentiana sino-ornata,* or many bulbs, simply fall apart when they are lifted from the ground, presenting you with innumerable ready-made plants. Others need prising apart: fingers can be used for this operation, but it may be necessary to resort to the knife in some plants such as hostas. Make certain that each division has a growing point and roots.

A cross between division and a cutting is the so-called 'Irishman's cutting' which is a piece of stem with roots, too small to be regarded as a plant, removed from the side of the plant and then potted up as a rooted cutting.

Layering

This is not quite so common in alpine gardening, but basically it consists of pinning a stem of a plant to the ground so that it produces roots and eventually, when severed from its parent, a new plant. This is most frequently done with shrubby plants that are difficult to strike from cuttings, but it is also carried out on herbaceous material such as some of the *Dianthus.*

The procedure is quite simple, a long branch is selected and split on the underside at about half-way along its length. This slit is then placed in a depression in the soil filled with potting compost. The layer is kept in place with either a stone or a pin of some sort. A stone has the advantage of not only keeping the layer in place but keeping it cool and moist. It should always be kept moist.

It can take a long time for some of the woody subjects to layer, years in some cases, but eventually roots will form and the layer can be cut from the parent plant. It is a good idea to layer some of the slow-growing plants even if you have no immediate requirements. It takes a little time to prepare a layer and there will doubtless come a time when you will congratulate yourself on your forethought.

Layering

Grafting

There are some woody plants that are difficult to propagate or are extremely slow to do so (for example some of the daphnes and conifers) and the best way to tackle these is by grafting. Basically this involves taking a shoot (the scion) from the plant you want to grow and 'welding' it on to the rootstock of another, more readily grown species. For example, *Daphne petraea* 'Grandiflora' is normally grafted on to the rootstock of *Daphne mezereum,* which can easily be grown from seed.

There are several types of graft. The simplest, the side graft, is to cut diagonally through both the scion and the stock and bind them together with grafting tape. The saddle graft is another simple and popular method. Here an inverted 'V' is cut in the scion with a matching inverted 'V' on the stock, both are united and again bound. The wedge graft is useful when the scion is narrower than the stock. This is the reverse of the saddle graft in that it is a 'V' rather than an inverted 'V' that is its basis. It is essential that the cambium layer (the outer ring where growth takes place) of each part comes in contact with each other. If the stock and scion are of different diameter, then the scion should be to one side ensuring that contact is made. This must be carefully bound with tape to ensure that the graft does not move to prevent water getting into and staying in the 'V', causing rot.

There are several other methods of producing a graft. The above will be sufficient for most requirements of alpine gardeners but this is a specialist technique and if it is decided to go into it in depth then a book specialising on the subject is advised.

Micropropagation

This is one of the latest ways of propagating plants. This is a complicated method that involves producing plants from just a few cells or the growing tips of the plant. These cells are multiplied up in laboratory conditions until it becomes a recognisable plant and then more conventional procedures take over. It is now used commercially to produce vast quantities of difficult to propagate plants (such as orchids). Micropropagation involves the use of glass tubes and sterile conditions rather than frames and compost and as yet is way beyond the means of amateur growers, although some are dabbling in it. It is worth knowing what it is because it will crop up in conversation or in literature, but as a means of producing plants in the garden it is not important. These techniques are sometimes also known as meristem culture or tissue culture.

Plants from the wild

Once upon a time it was very common practice to consider digging up plants in the wild as a means of increasing stock. This is now very severely frowned on, with very good reason. Natural habitats are under threat from many different sources: pollution, physical destruction (roads, ski runs, overgrazing), tourism and over-collecting. Important as the others are, it is the last mentioned which concerns us here. Many plants have been wiped out in the wild by over-zealous collecting. Tropical orchids are an obvious example, but in our field the delightful vivid-blue *Tecophilaea* has been collected out of existence from its native mountains in Chile. Many, many other plants are nearing that position as pressures increase. Bulbs in particular seem vulnerable. Our thirst for cyclamen means the wholesale destruction of complete areas in Turkey as millions of bulbs are sent into Europe, quite illegally, each year.

It might seem insignificant to dig up one plant somewhere in the mountains while you are on holiday, but the number of people doing this is increasing and the plants are decreasing. The sad thing is that few of these plants will survive the journey home or get the aftercare if they do. Overheard remarks such as 'I know I won't be able to get this home but I am going to try' shows a totally irresponsible attitude and one which we will all regret in the long term.

Perhaps if plant losses were only due to the relatively small activity of collectors then the situation would not be too bad, but it must be taken into consideration along with all the other factors. The effects of things such as overgrazing, road construction, holiday homes and so on, all compound to make the continued existence of many plants quite perilous. Even in the high mountains where these pressures have not arrived, airborne pollution is tipping the delicate balance.

Although some people object, it is still considered permissible to collect seed from the wild if one is not too greedy. As long as the plant is not rare and depends on its seed for survival then a few seed can be brought back. Even from organised plant collecting expeditions, seed is now the normal way of getting plants into cultivation; the plants themselves are left for other people to enjoy.

Any seed that is collected in the wild should be accompanied by notes saying where it was collected and in what kind of conditions the plant was growing. This is important so that the seed, and subsequent seedlings, can be given the right kind of conditions to ensure their survival. Having collected the seed there is an onus to ensure that as many plants are raised as possible to make the best use of what, after all, is a precious resource. Spread the plants around to other people so that even if yours die there will be the chance that somebody else's will survive. In this way plants enter general cultivation and their future is to a certain extent safeguarded, a vindication of collecting the seed in the first place.

Collect seed, yes, but do leave the plants for others to enjoy.

Plant Care

It is one thing buying a plant and putting it in the ground and another to keep it flourishing and looking happy.

Buying plants

As will have been discovered on the way through this book, there are three ways of acquiring plants: purchase, gift or propagation. (There is a fourth, which unfortunately is becoming quite prevalent — theft. Do not remove plants, cuttings or seed without the owner's permission. The last two are bad enough, but theft of plants from fellow enthusiasts' gardens and even from their alpine houses is the lowest to which any gardener can sink.)

Throughout your life as an alpine gardener you will always buy plants, possibly more when you are first setting out than later on. Go easy to start with, do not rush to buy the difficult and the rare. The simple ones are just as beautiful and will present far less disappointments. With knowledge gained from these you can progress.

If you follow advice and start with the simple ones then these can be generally purchased from your nearest alpine nursery. One big advantage of this is the advice you can get from the nurseryman. There is not much money made in the nursery trade (as opposed to the garden centre world), most do it for their love of plants and they are always willing to talk about your purchases (but do not outstay your welcome, they are busy people). During these visits to the nursery you will see plants growing and gain from the nurseryman's knowledge. It is a rare alpine gardener who does not resolve after one of these visits that he should dig up the rest of the vegetable plot and turn it into yet another raised bed.

Nursery catalogues are another source of information about plants and are well worth acquiring. Print and postage costs being what they are these days, most nurserymen have now to charge for their catalogues, but they are usually well worth the small outlay. When ordering from a catalogue it is wise to send an open cheque limited to a certain sum, so that if the plants are not available the nurseryman can adjust the total cost accordingly. Alternatively give plenty of second choices.

Most plants are sent out in the spring or autumn. If you are going to be away, let the nurseryman know when you order, otherwise you might return to find a parcel of dead plants on the doorstep. When the plants arrive unpack them and put them in a cool shady position, watering if need be, for a few days. If the plants have been bare-rooted, i.e. taken out of their pots, they should be potted up straightaway and then dealt with in the same fashion. The plants can be then hardened off and planted out.

If it is intended to continue the plants in pots, either permanently or, if they are small, until they are big enough to plant out, then it is wise to repot the plants on receipt, removing most of the compost and using your own mix and then proceed as you would for any potted-on plant.

Do not be in too much of a rush to plant out; be certain that you have a flourishing plant before you thrust it into the competitive outside world.

Siting plants

Once the plant has been bought the most crucial consideration is its siting. As explained in previous chapters the plant must be in the type of soil it likes: well-drained, moist or lime-free for instance, and it must be in the kind of environment that it likes: sunny, part shade, full shade, cool, hot, and so on.

Gardening is an art that is mastered by getting your hands dirty and gaining experience, but in alpine gardening it also involves reading and, occasionally, some research. If you buy a plant or raise one from seed with which you are unfamiliar, then it is essential to find out what conditions it requires; i.e. in what conditions it grows in the wild. For a bought plant perhaps the seller will be able to tell you, but it is more difficult with plants raised from seed. It may be you have a knowledgeable friend who can help, but the most common source are reference books. This book will help many plants but there are potentially thousands and thousands of plants you can grow (the Alpine Garden Society Seed List runs to nearly 5,000 items each year and this is only the tip of the iceberg). Arm yourself with one or two good reference books (a list is given at the end of this book). It may seem that this is expensive but the money will be more than saved on plants that are not lost by knowing the correct conditions.

The all-round alpine gardener will create as many different types of conditions and microclimates as he can in his garden and place his plants accordingly; the plant in the right place is off to a very good start.

Labels and records

Having planted your plant the next thing to do is to label it. This may seem trivial, but you will soon discover that it is a very important process for a variety of reasons. The first is that you will soon forget what the plant is, and second where it is. Later will come other queries, often in reply to questions from visitors, such as when your plant was acquired and from where.

All this information can be conveniently written on to a label. I normally use both sides of a label with details of the plant's origin written on the back. On the front I give the name of the plant in full, date of purchase (or sowing if raised from seed). The collector's number should be included if the plant was raised from a seed collected in the wild.

Start writing the information from the top, not the pointed end, of the label. This makes it easier to read when it is stuck in the earth.

There are several types of label that can be used but, alas, there seems to be no satisfactory one at the moment. Lead labels were once the accepted method, but these died out when it became impossible to get the lead blanks and the machines that printed the labels had become very expensive. Aluminium labels then became very popular and were very satisfactory. Unfortunately the company making them eventually ceased trading, but many alpine gardeners still have quantities of these and they are as precious as gold dust. There is a new firm that makes aluminium labels but they are nearly ten times the original price and not such good labels, so they are mostly avoided (not many people like to use labels that cost more than the plant it is identifying!).

The most commonly available at the moment are strips of white plastic. These will take either a water-proof ink or pencil. I find the latter the most satisfactory. Unfortunately the plastic becomes brittle and snaps after a year or so in the ground. Blackbirds also seem to delight in pulling them up. There is an alternative plastic which is coated with a black paint. The name of the plant is scratched through this to the white plastic beneath. They are not quite so conspicuous in the border (in

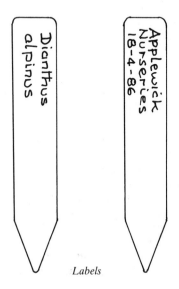

Labels

winter the bed looks less like a graveyard), birds leave them alone and they are more durable. Unfortunately only one side is coated so if you use both sides a pencil is needed for one of them and the provided stylus for the other.

Another advantage of the old aluminium labels was that one end could easily be wrapped around a galvanised piece of wire which anchored them firmly in the ground. Plastic labels do tend to wander and have to be tied to the wire.

Other records can include the same information recorded in a book. This can be a permanent record which is updated each time the plant is repotted, cuttings taken or even the time of flowering each year. The big advantage of this kind of record is that the plant has to be keenly observed to get the information in the first place, and a great deal of detail can be collected over the years giving the recorder an intimate knowledge of his plants.

Watering

This subject has been dealt with at length under rock gardens and the alpine house. I do not intend to go into it again, except to reiterate that alpine plants, contrary to what some people say, do need water. They need it regularly and in reasonable quantity, but the soil or compost must be free-draining to prevent stagnant water lying around.

Feeding

Again this has been dealt with under appropriate areas. Do not overfeed and avoid nitrogen-rich fertilisers.

Mulch

The rock garden, raised beds, troughs and pots in the alpine house should all have a gravel or stone chipping mulch applied to the whole area. This helps to prevent panning when it rains or when the bed is watered, to give an even watering, to conserve moisture, keep the neck of the plant dry, suppress weeds and to give a good background against which to see the plants. The chippings should reflect the local stone, and that used in the bed. Do not use limestone chippings on calcifuges (lime-haters). Each year, check the mulch and top up if necessary.

Wood bark or peat can be used as a mulch on peat beds.

Maintenance

All beds should be regularly weeded; if left too long it then becomes an uphill task to regain control and the ultimate solution is to scrap any badly infected bed and start again. Avoid using weedkiller, except possibly in the initial clearance of the site.

Remove any dead or broken material from the plants and remove any debris such as dead leaves, blown paper, and so on. Good hygiene in the garden and in the alpine house will help prevent disease and pests.

Regularly take cuttings and sow seed of some of the more precious of your plants. This is a safeguard against losing them through old age, disease or a harsh winter. It also helps if you give offspring to friends, then if you lose your only plant or your entire stock through disease or disaster, somebody somewhere still has a plant and it gives you a chance of starting again.

In the winter cover with a sheet of glass any plants that might suffer from excessive cold or moisture. But make certain that the air can flow around them;

stagnant air is liable to make things worse. Polythene lights can be made to cover whole areas of raised beds.

Pests and Diseases

Nature is very diverse in its animal and plant life. The one thing they all have in common is the ability to survive even if this means that they have to eat one of their neighbours to do so. The neighbours, in turn, throw up some form of defence mechanism, even if it is sheer numbers, otherwise it would not survive. In the garden we see this battle going on and tend to come down on the side of the hunted and try to improve their chances. Many gardeners take any attack on their plants very personally: an earwig nibbling a dahlia is biting them, a sparrow pulling a crocus to pieces can cause a fit.

In the open garden, alpines tend to be able to look after themselves better than many other sections of the plant community. It would be naïve to say that there are no problems, but many alpine gardeners rarely have to resort to chemical warfare. The alpine house presents a different problem. Here the conditions are just right for the predators; often they can overwinter in comfort; and the plants may have succulent growth which is just suited to all forms of attack from both pests and diseases. But, again, with any luck and good management, this need not be too serious.

One of the most important factors in the battle against pests and diseases is good hygiene. Make certain that all rotting and dead vegetation is removed. Check all plants you bring into the garden thoroughly to make certain they are harbouring no pests. Some gardeners go to the extreme of removing all soil from any introduced plants and destroying it and then repotting the plants in their own pest-free compost. This kind of vigilance pays off. For example vine weevil is one of the worst pests in the alpine garden and alpine house where it does a great deal of damage. The adult cannot fly and it is nearly always introduced at the larva stage in pots of plants where it lives on the roots. If every plant is thoroughly checked, the chances of keeping this menace out are increased.

Pests

These can conveniently be divided into animal and insect pests. The alpine house is easily dealt with here as it is possible to cover all openings with a wire mesh which will allow free circulation of air and yet impede the entrance of domestic and wild animals and birds. Barriers, in the form of fences, can be put up around the garden to keep out some of the pests such as rabbits and deer. In the case of the former, the wire should be dug into the ground to prevent their burrowing under it. Deer fencing should be at least 2.4m (8ft) high to prevent the deer from jumping it. Mice do a lot of damage to bulbs. Trapping can be effective in keeping numbers down to reasonable proportions. Cats also help with their control but then they can be a nuisance in their own right! Moles can be a nuisance, too, not damaging the plants directly, but burrowing beneath them leaving their roots dangling in a dry space. None of the folklore remedies work; the only way is to trap or get in a specialist firm who will poison them.

Poisoning is not the answer to all problems, particularly where domestic pets are concerned of course. Wire-netting can be placed over newly cultivated and planted areas to discourage cats and dogs. There are powders that are supposed to keep them away, but verbal abuse seems to be the universal solution.

Birds present a problem. Some, such as blackbirds, wreck cushion plants in their search for grubs, others, e.g. bullfinches, eat out the buds, yet others, such as pheasants, gorge themselves on the plants. Some, sparrows in particular, seem to destroy just for the sake of it, although there must be some practical explanation. Most of these attacks seem to come during the late winter when other foodstuff is in short supply. If the attacks are bad it might become necessary to cover the plants with netting or with strands of black cotton until the threat is past. Some years are worse than others, yet it does not seem to relate to the weather. For all the harm they do, birds also help the gardener by eating other pests, such as aphids and caterpillars, often to the extent of controlling them.

Slugs and snails are the bane of any gardener's life. Good hygiene helps as it removes a lot of the places where slugs will hide, under leaves for example. There is a traditional method of surrounding the plants with grit or ashes, on the theory that the slimy creatures will not like the abrasive surface. Alas this is theory rather than practice; I have often seen them walking (if that is the correct word) across large areas of sharp grit in both the alpine house and in the open garden to get to plants.

There seems to be only two effective ways: slug bait and fingers. Many people, particularly with pets, are against using slug bait. If used carefully following the directions on the packet it should be safe for all except slugs and snails. It is the most effective way of clearing an area, at least for a while. There are now new baits which claim not to harm animals and pets. The other method is to go out late at night with a torch and pick off the slugs as they feed, dropping them into a jar of water to which a little washing-up liquid has been added. After a few nights the slugs will have been reduced to manageable proportions.

Another method is to put up a barricade around susceptible plants. A lemonade bottle with the top and bottom cut off will suffice, but this will in no way reduce the slug population and they will feed elsewhere. The other method is to put down 'traps' in the form of empty grapefruit skins, which offer the slugs a refuge during daylight hours. These are checked every day and emptied of their slimy inhabitants.

Moving down the scale we come to the insect pests; often unseen until the damage is done. The problem is worst in the enclosed environment of the alpine house, where the conditions are not only just right for growing plants but for breeding pests as well; in the open garden, unless there is a severe attack from some insect one can usually live with the situation.

I am sorry to keep stressing this point, but hygiene is again one of the best weapons of defence. The chances of attack are reduced if there is nowhere for the pests to live amongst dead and rotting vegetation. In order to monitor what is going on it is a good idea to place a yellow bowl of water on the bench. This has the facility of attracting insects and, as well as killing a few off, it will let you know what pests are around so that you can take evasive action before the outbreak becomes too serious. The water should be changed regularly otherwise it gets rather foul.

There are several ways of tackling the insect problem. Chemical warfare is the most obvious. If the manufacturer's instructions are followed there should be no danger to other animals, but and it is a big but, quite a number of alpines object to being subjected to the chemical and others, particularly cushion plants and some with rosettes, do not like being made wet with spray and are likely to rot.

Some growers add a weak solution of a systemic insecticide to every other watering and claim that this does no harm to the plants and wards off any insect attacks. Two or three different brands are used in rotation to reduce the risk of immunity building up in the insects. Other growers do not like using any chemicals until it is necessary, i.e. once the attack has begun. Others refuse to use any chemicals at all and rely on using their fingers or tweezers to pick off all the greenfly, for example.

There have been two other innovations recently. The first is just a new version of an old device, namely the flypaper. The current version is a yellow plastic sheet impregnated with a chemical and sticky substance which attracts and then kills the insects. This is simply hung in the alpine house, preferably out of the way of the owner's head. The other method is biological control. It is becoming increasingly possible to buy through the post batches of insects that are predators on your particular pests. A simple example of this is the introduction of ladybirds or lacewings when there is a greenfly outbreak. This technique is still in its infancy but some growers are already using it.

Of the several methods described, chemicals are probably the most effective, but many gardeners are becoming increasingly concerned about their use. The decision is yours.

The most worrying of pests is the vine weevil. This is troublesome both as a larva and as an adult. In its latter manifestation it only chews leaves and flowers, which although annoying is not usually fatal to the plane, but as a larva it is. Here, as a small white grub, curled up like a horshoe, it chews through the roots of many types of plant. Favourite on its menu are primulas, geraniums and cyclamen. The first sign of its presence is when the plant suddenly wilts and dies. Nothing can be done at this stage as the plant has usually lost most if not all of its roots.

It is equally at home in the garden or the alpine house. Control is not very easy, as the only chemical, aldrin, that had any real effect on it is now banned. Some people have claimed success with HCH (UK), either spraying to kill the adults or by mixing it as dust into the compost of pots or the soil layer in the open garden. The adults can walk but not fly, so introduction is usually within a pot containing a plant from another garden. Thorough checking of all such pots may prevent its appearance. If the soil is friable, the grubs can be sifted out in any infected areas. Another method often proposed is to catch the adults at night when they are chewing leaves. This is easier said than done; the insect immediately drops to the ground when disturbed and it is difficult to find the long-snouted beasts in the soil. A sheet of white paper can be put on the ground and the plant shaken, after which you can wreak whatever vengeance takes your fancy.

There are other root-chewing larvae such as leather-jackets, wireworms and cock-chafers. These do not normally exist in such numbers as the vine weevil. If they do become a menace then HCH can again be incorporated in the soil of the infected area.

Caterpillars can be a nuisance, often not seen, because of their camouflage, until after the damage is done. The most effective control is to go out after dark with a torch and pick the offending animals from the plants. The simple operation is usually sufficient to keep the problem under control, indeed, nighttime visits to the alpine house, frames and garden can solve a lot of the pest problems. If the infestation of caterpillars is too great to be tackled in this way then chemical control can be easily achieved.

Commonest of the pests is the aphid, commonly known as the greenfly or blackfly. They cause two different types of problem; they damage the plants and they are able to transmit virus infections from other plants. They are often hidden down in the axils of the plants and their sticky secretion is the first sign of their presence. Being the most common of pests there is a wide selection of insecticides to control them. They can also be controlled by crushing between the fingers or tweezers; a messy but effective method. They are at their worse in the alpine house, only serious outbreaks in the open garden need attention; birds, lacewings and ladybirds will normally keep them under control.

There are other sap-sucking insects besides aphids; these include capsid bugs, leafhoppers, mealy bugs and whiteflies. Chemical control is the most effective method of dealing with these but whitefly can effectively be dealt with by the modern equivalent of flypapers.

Red spider mites are another scourge of the alpine house, particularly in hot dry summers. These are so small that they are difficult to see. The results of their handiwork can be seen though: the leaves of a plant become yellow speckled before turning yellow and eventually dropping off. They do not like moist, humid conditions and a wet plunge is a good precaution against attacks.

Ants can be a nuisance in dry, well-drained areas and, since rock gardens are constructed to reproduce these conditions, they are often present. Plants in their immediate vicinity are often killed, either as a result of their tunnelling activities or by direct damage to the roots and the introduction of disease. Chemical control is quite easy and effective.

Diseases

On the whole alpine plants are not prone to disease. The most likely to succumb are those that have been overfed and are full of lush succulent growth. The most common diseases are fungal and viral diseases. Botrytis (grey mould) is probably the disease that most people have problems with. Prevention is the key note. Removal of all rotting material and the free circulation of air will do a lot in keeping botrytis under control. Under humid conditions a fungicide may be necessary to prevent outbreaks of this and other fungal diseases such as mildews. Viral diseases are more difficult to control. Their introduction is often through the presence of another virally affected plant or through sap-sucking insects such as aphids. Checking all new plants thoroughly and keeping aphids under control will go a long way to keeping the plants virus-free.

The other type of diseases are caused by deficiency or presence of various minerals. Thus a rhododendron will soon show its displeasure of being planted on chalk, as it induces lime chlorosis. This can be redressed by adding iron in the form of sequestrene to the soil, but on strongly alkaline soils it is not worth it. If you live on pure chalk either give up the idea of growing lime-haters, such as the ericaceae (there are plenty of other interesting plants), or construct special raised beds which are free of lime. Nutrient deficient diseases can be solved by dressing with a general fertiliser. Most of these deficiencies manifest themselves by yellowing of the leaves. A soil test will show you what is missing.

A dismal section, but pests and diseases are not too serious a problem for the alpine gardener, particularly one who takes a few simple precautions, in particular good hygiene and keen observation.

6 Plants

Nomenclature

Many people find that Latin plant names are baffling and very difficult to understand and remember. The main thing is not to worry about it; gradually names will sink in and you will become accustomed to using them. After all, Latin names such as geranium, delphinium, chrysanthemum, and many more, are all very familiar even to non-gardeners. These trip off the tongue quite readily although they are unlike any other words in everyday speech. It is often the pronunciation, rather than the words themselves, that worry some people. Again there is no need to worry; there are several different ways of pronouncing most names and yours is likely to be as valid as anybody else's. I have had a conversation with three eminent growers in which they were all pronouncing the same plant differently. If you ever discuss plants with foreigners you will realise that there are even more ways of pronouncing Latin. Just pronounce it with confidence in the way you think it should be said and all will be well.

Latin was chosen for names given to plants as it is an international language; in other words the names are valid for all countries, no matter what is the native language. The other international aspect of plants is the system of classification employed. Classification helps to bring order to the thousands of different plants by grouping them by some common features. We will omit some of the broader groupings and move straight to the level of families. The plant world is divided into a series of families, all the plants in one family having certain characteristics which differentiate it from another family. These characteristics, and those of the genera which are mentioned in a moment, are always attributes of the flower, seed or fruit. Family names end in 'ae' and in publications are normally printed in ordinary type, for example the buttercup family is known as the Ranunculaceae.

Within each family are a number of genera (singular: genus). Each genus is bound together by a set of characteristics which differentiate it from other genera within the family. Generic names have a variety of endings and are given in *italic type*. It is always the first in the complete name. Although given first, it is, in a way, the equivalent to the plant's surname. Thus within the Ranunculaceae there are, amongst others, the *Delphinium, Clematis, Aquilegia, Anemone* and *Ranunculus* genera.

Within each genus is a number of species. This is always represented as the second element of the name, e.g. *montana* in *Clematis montana,* and can be considered equivalent to the plant's forename. The specific name is usually one of three types: descriptive, e.g. *Alyssum spinosum* (spiny alyssum), after a person, e.g. *Primula forrestii* (named after George Forrest) or a place, e.g. *Erodium corsicum* (from Corsica). Gradually a lot of these specific names will become familiar as they crop up in many different genera. For example *depressus* always means flattened (or depressed) wherever it occurs. Similarly *grandiflorus* means large-flowered, *minor*, small, and so on.

In articles and books, when there are several species of the same genus it is conventional to replace the generic name by its initial after its first appearance. So it would now be legitimate to write *E. macradenum* for *Erodium macradenum* as *Erodium* was mentioned in the previous paragraph. Another convention is to make the ending of the specific name agree in gender with the generic name, e.g. *Erinus alpinus* and *Linaria alpina*. Sometimes they do not appear to agree (e.g. *Phyteuma comosum*) because the generic word is Greek rather than Latin!

Things are further complicated by there often being one or more extra elements in a name. It is sometimes thought necessary to subdivide a species even further into subspecies, and these names are usually preceded by the abbreviation 'ssp.' or 'subsp.' e.g. *Crocus biflorus* subsp. *adamii*. If there has already been a reference to *Crocus biflorus* then this may be abbreviated to *C.b. adamii*. When the variation is not important enough to warrant subspecific rank then it is termed a variety (var.), e.g. *Crocus pestalozzae* var. *caeruleus*. Both subspecies and variety are used of a plant in the wild, in cultivation it is given a cultivar name. This is given in ordinary type between single quotation marks, e.g. *Crocus chrysanthus* 'Lady Killer'.

Hybrids between two species are given in the form *Primula edgeworthii* × *irregularis* where *P. edgeworthii* was the seed parent and *P. irregularis* was the pollen parent. In cultivation it is often impossible to tell the parentage of a hybrid and so a cross may just be given a hybrid name, e.g. *Primula* 'Broxbourne'. In older publications this may be seen as *Primula* × 'Broxbourne'. The other type of hybrid that is occasionally seen is the bigeneric hybrid which occurs between two different genera rather than two different species within a genus. Here the × is given first, followed by a combination of the two generic names. Thus × *Gaulnettya wisleyensis* is a cross between *Gaultheria shallon* and *Pernyetta mucronata*.

There are a few minor variations on the above, but if you have followed the argument thus far, you should have no difficulty in understanding names; but the problem still remains on how to remember them. Time and experience will tell, but there is one point which might help and that is the meaning of the name. If you buy a dictionary of plant names you will soon begin to realise what certain words mean. For example *albus* (*alba* or *album*, depending on gender) means white and is usually only used on white-flowered (or sometimes white-leaved) plants. So if you remember that *Pulsatilla alba* is the white-flowered pulsatilla you are on the right road. Similarly remember *Erodium corsicum* as the Corsican erodium and soon the Latin name will become familiar enough to drop the English version. All names mean something even those terrible ones named after Russian or East European botanists or place names. Try getting your tongue around *Anemone tschernjaewii*, or, even better, *Corydalis hsiaowutaishanensis*! Fortunately, as you will find, these are the exceptions rather than the rule.

A–Z of Plants

There is no space to give a complete list of alpines that you are likely to come across. There is another book in this series (*A Manual of Alpine and Rock Garden Plants*) which is intended to give you a fuller description of the species you may want to grow. Here I have just given a brief outline of the various genera, including a description and the typical conditions and requirements of their species. This should be adequate to help you with any strange plants that you may acquire.

The heights given are those for the plants normally grown as alpines. There are often others in the genus which are much taller. Where more than one method of propagation is given the first is usually the preferred technique. Where rock garden is specified, the plant is also suitable for raised beds.

In order to help the reader understand the requirements of the species described, a simple system of symbols has been employed as follows:

○ plants require full sun
◑ plants require shade or half-shade
▢ plants require an acid soil
☆ easy and especially recommended to the beginner
▲ difficult species to cultivate successfully

Acaena (Rosaceae) ○☆
Mainly from New Zealand. 15cm (6in) carpeters with very good foliage and burr-like flower heads. May be invasive, forming large mats but easy attractive plants for beginners. Propagate by rooted pieces or seed.

Acantholimon (Plumbaginaceae) ○
A large genus from Greece eastwards to Tibet. Spiny cushions with 'everlasting' white, pink or purple flowers in summer, up to 15cm (6in). Can be grown in a hot sunny position or in the alpine house. Requires good drainage and resents moving. Propagate by seed or cuttings.

Achillea (Compositae) ○☆
Rock forms up to 25cm (10in). Mainly grown as foliage plants in a well-drained position in the rock garden. Often deeply cut, silvery foliage. Yellow or white flowers in summer. Propagate by cuttings, division or seed.

Aciphylla (Umbelliferae) ○
Mainly from New Zealand. Grown mostly for their pointed leaves. Some will grow outside in well-drained positions, others are a little tender and need glass protection. Propagate by seed.

Aconitum (Ranunculaceae) Monkshood ○◑
A few small enough for the rock garden; taller ones can be grown in shade or peat bed. Mainly blue or white; summer flowering. Propagate by seed or root cuttings.

Adiatum (Polypodiaceae) Maidenhair fern ○◑
Up to 60cm (2 ft). A fern for the woodland garden and back of the peat bed. Propagate by division in spring.

Adonis (Ranunculaceae) ○◑
Herbaceous plants from around the world. Large, yellow buttercup-like flowers, in early summer, above finely cut foliage; up to 30cm (1ft). Will do well in a peat bed or rock gargen. Propagate by seed or division in early spring.

Aethionema (Cruciferae) ○☆
Shrubby plants from Mediterranean area. Four-petalled, pink flowers in early summer; up to 23cm (9in). Sunny well-drained position. Propagate by seed; will self-sow.

Ajuga (Labiatae) Bugle ○◑☆
Low carpeters with up to 15cm (6in) spikes of blue or purple flowers. Some grown

for foliage coloration. Good ground-cover plant; can be invasive. Propagate by division or seed.

Alchemilla (Rosaceae) ○◗☆
World-wide plants, some shorter ones suitable for the rock garden, mainly grown for the foliage. Hummocks of roundish or palmately lobed leaves with a froth of green flowers. For the rock garden or peat bed. Propagate by seed or division; some self-sow.

Alkanna (Boraginaceae) ○
Blue-flowered plants from the Mediterranean and Near East. Grow in rock garden in sunny position or in alpine house. Propagate by seed.

Allium (Liliaceae) Onions ○
Large genus of bulbs, many of which are suitable for the rock garden. Round or loose heads of white, red, pink, purple, blue or yellow flowers; early summer to late autumn flowering. Some are invasive self-seeders (avoid *A. moly* and *A. pulchellum*). Propagate by seed or division of the bulbs.

Alstroemeria (Amaryllidaceae) ○
Large genus of bulbs from South America. Many slightly tender and need protection of alpine house or bulb frame. Rare but increasing numbers in cultivation.

Alyssum (Cruciferae) ○☆
Up to 23cm (9in) hummocks of four-petalled yellow flowers in the spring or early summer. Sunny spots in rock gardens. Propagate by cuttings or seed.

Anacyclus (Compositae) ○☆
Daisy-like flowers from the Mediterranean region, best ones from the Atlas Mountains. Prostrate with finely cut leaves; white flowers with red-backed petals, in summer. Sunny spot with sharp drainage. Propagate by seed or cuttings.

Anagalis (Primulaceae) ○
Wide distribution including Britain (Scarlet Pimpernel). Bright red, pink or blue flowers on sprawling plants; summer flowering. Any good garden soil. Propagate by seed or cuttings.

Anchusa (Boraginaceae) ○
There is only one species, from Crete, suitable for alpine growers, *A. caespitosa*. Stalkless deep blue, white-eyed flowers in a rosette of strap-like leaves; summer flowering; 2.5–5cm (1–2in) high. Best grown in the alpine house in deep pots, but will grow in sunny well-drained position. Propagate by root cuttings or seed.

Andromeda (Ericaceae) ◗☆▢
Small shrubs up to 45cm (18in). Pink or white urn- or bell-shaped flowers; summer flowering. Dislikes lime and prefers shade. Ideal for the peat garden. Propagate by summer cuttings.

Androsace (Primulaceae) ○☆▲
A large genus spreading around the nothern hemisphere. Small cushion- or mat-forming plants that generally dislike the wet. Flowers pink or white, sometimes yellow-eyed, from early summer to autumn. Many can only be grown in the alpine house although some can be grown outside. Some are easy for the beginner (e.g.

AA. lanuginosa, sarmentosa and *sempervivoides*), others are more difficult, and some only for the specialist. All need sunny well-drained position. Propagate by seed or cuttings. See AGS publication *Androsace* for detailed cultivation.

Anemone (Ranunculaceae) ○◑☆
World-wide distribution. Low plants, up to 30cm (12in), some spreading but rarely invasive. White, blue, yellow or pink flowers mainly in the spring. Majority like woodland conditions so suitable for the peat garden. Propagate by division or seed.

Anemonella (Ranunculaceae) ○◑
A one species (*A. thalictroides*) genus from North America. A delicate white or pink flower on 15cm (6in) stem, in spring. Woodlander so suitable for the peat bed; gently spreading; does not like disturbance. Propagate by seed.

Antennaria (Compositae) ○
World-wide distribution. Mat-forming silver- or grey-leaved plants with 'everlasting' flowers of white to dark pink; up to 10cm (4in). Can be used as ground cover. Prefers sunny well drained position. Propagate by division.

Anthemis (Compositae) ○
From Europe, Africa and Asia. White daisy-flowered plants mainly grown for their deeply cut silvery foliage; up to 30cm (12in). Likes sunny well-drained position. Propagate by cuttings.

Anthericum (Liliaceae) ○☆
Large genus of bulbous plants from Europe, Africa and America of which one, *A. liliago,* is commonly grown. 30–45cm (12–18in) high, with white starry flowers; summer flowering. Any good soil in the sun. Propagate by seed or division.

Antirrhinum (Scrophulariaceae) ○
European. Short-lived perennials with pouched, snapdragon flowers in a variety of colours; early summer flowering. Requires sunny free-draining soil in a sheltered position. Propagate by seed.

Aquilegia (Ranunculaceae) Columbine ○☆
Widespread, large genus from northern hemisphere. Attractive flowers in wide colour range, although alpine species mainly blue and white. Up to 30cm (12in) for alpine forms; late spring and summer flowering. Propagate by seed. Open pollinated forms may form hybrids. Most are easy for beginners.

Arabis (Cruciferae) ○☆
Low, up to 7.5cm (3in), plants with four-petalled flowers of white or shades of pink; leaves often hairy. From Europe and America. Sunny position in well-drained soil. Propagate by seed or cuttings. Most are easy for beginners.

Arctostaphylos (Ericaceae) ○◑☐
Low carpeting shrubs from Europe and North America. Urn-shaped flowers of pink or white, with brilliant red berries; 15cm (6in) high; summer flowering. Spreads making good ground cover. Propagate by cuttings or seed.

Arenaria (Caryophyllaceae) ○
Widespread in northern hemisphere. Low, up to 15cm (6in), mat-forming plants. Small white flowers from early summer onwards. Likes sunny well-drained

position, except *A. balearica* which prefers cool moist conditions. Propagate by division or seed.

Arisaema (Araceae) ◑
Large genus mainly from Asia which is becoming increasingly popular. Curious plants, related to the British native arum, with a hood, often strangely coloured, hanging over the spadix. Up to 30cm (2ft). Likes shady cool conditions; ideal for the peat bed. Some are tender. Propagate by seed.

Arisarum (Araceae) ◑☆
Small genus of which only *A. proboscideum* is of interest. Curious spathes like mousetails appear from the spear-shaped leaves in spring; 10cm (4in). Shady moist position; ideal for the peat garden. Propagate by division.

Armeria (Plumbaginaceae) Thrift ○☆
Cushions of narrow, stiff leaves with balls of papery flowers, their colour being shades of pink or white, from early summer, up to 20cm (8in). Needs sunny position with well-drained soil. Propagate by seed or cuttings.

Arnebia (Boraginacea) ○☆
Only one species of general interest, *A. echioides* (Prophet Flower). Five yellow flowers with a brown-black spot at the base of each; summer flowering; 23cm (9in). Sunny well-drained position. Propagate by division in spring or root cuttings over winter.

Arnica (Compositeae) ○▢
Small genus from Europe and North America. Large yellow daisy flowers on stems up to 25cm (10in) high; early summer flowering. Prefers a lime-free soil. Propagate by division or seed.

Artemisia (Compositae) ○☆
Northern hemisphere distribution. Mostly aromatic, silver-leaved plants, used mainly for their foliage, which is often finely cut. Flowers are rayless and usually brown or yellow. Up to 30cm (12in). Sunny, well-drained position. Propagate by cuttings.

Arum (Araceae) ◑
From Europe, particularly the Mediterranean region. Colourful flowering spikes, the spadix, enclosed in a hooded sheath (the spathe). Mainly grow in woodland conditions and therefore good for the peat bed, except *A. creticum* which prefers a sunny position. 30cm (12in) or more. Propagate by seed.

Asarina (Scrophulariaceae) ◑
European. Mainly known through *A. procumbens*. Pale yellow snapdragon-type flowers on sticky trailing stems. Useful for shady positions, which can be quite dry. Propagate by seed; will self-sow.

Asperula (Rubiaceae) ○
A few of this large genus are suitable for the rock garden or alpine house. The leaves are in whorls about the stem, sometimes they are quite woolly. Very small tubular flowers of mainly pink, but also white and yellow. Prefers position with maximum light but not too hot, in well-drained soil. Woolly-leaved species hate the wet and need winter protection. Propagate by division, seed or cuttings.

Asphodelus (Liliaceae) ○
The only suitable species is *A. acaulis* from the Atlas Mountains. Narrow leaves cup almost stemless, pink tubular flowers. Does best in the alpine house where it flowers in late winter, but can have sheltered sunny position in well-drained soil in the rock garden. Propagate by division or seed.

Asplenium (Polypodiaceae) Spleenwort ◑
Very large genus (650 species) of ferns, many only 5–7cm (2–3in) high. Well-drained soil in light shade. Many very good for growing in walls or in shady crevices in the rock garden. Propagate by division or spores.

Aster (Compositae) ○☆
Large genus of over 500 species of which many are suitable for the alpine garden. Daisy-like flowers with a single row of petals in a variety of colours, with blue predominating, and a yellow centre; summer and autumn flowering. Heights vary from a few cm to tall herbaceous plants. Sunny well-drained position. Propagate by division or fresh seed.

Astilbe (Saxifragaceae) ◑
A few from North America and Asia are suitable for the alpine garden. Spires of pink, red, purple or white, up to 23cm (9in) in the dwarfer forms; summer and autumn flowering. Prefers cool, moist conditions; ideal for peat bed. Will take sun if soil kept moist. Propagate by division.

Astragalus (Leguminosae) ○
Very large genus of over 2,000 species found world-wide except Australia. Pea-like flowers in a range of colours; summer flowering; up to 30cm (12in). Sunny well-drained position. Dislikes disturbance. Propagate by seed.

Astrantia (Umbelliferae) ○◑☆
Small genus with one, *A. minor,* suitable for the rock garden. White and green flowers: what appear to be the petals are papery bracts forming a collar around the flower; summer flowering; 23cm (9in) high. Sun or light shade in a cool soil. Propagate by division or seed.

Aubrieta (Cruciferae) ○☆
A number of species as well as the well-known, sometimes brash hybrids. Mat-forming. Four-petalled flowers of blues and purples; spring flowering. Sunny well-drained position; grows well on walls. Propagate by cuttings or seed.

Bellis (Compositae) ○
European. Familiar as the small lawn daisies, there are a few other species for the rock garden. White or blue flowers; summer flowering. Sunny well-drained position. Propagate by division.

Bellum (Compositae) ○
Very similar to *Bellis.* European. Small white daisies; 2.5–5cm (1–2in) high. For a sunny position on the rock garden, with well-drained soil. Propagate by division.

Berberis (Berberidaceae) ◑☆
Large family of shrubs that contain some dwarf ones (up to 45cm (18in)) for the rock garden. Often grown as foliage plants but also has yellow or orange flowers in

early summer. Some are spiny. Any good soil, will take light shade. Propagate by cuttings or seed.

Bergenia (Saxifragaceae) ○◑

Most of these are too large for the alpine garden. Large green leaves and loose spikes of pink or white flowers; spring flowering. Will grow in any good soil in sun or shade, particularly useful for the latter. Propagate by division or seed.

Betula (Betulaceae) ◑

The only suitable one for the rock garden is *B. nana*. Reaches only 30cm (12in) in its compact forms. Catkins in spring and autumn tints later. Cool moist soil in rock garden or can be grown in alpine house. Propagate by seed or cuttings.

Biscutella (Cruciferae) ○

European and North Africa genus. Four-petalled yellow flowers. Some biennial. Needs sun and well-drained position on rock garden. Doubtful if worth growing.

Blettilla (Orchidaceae) ◑

A small genus of East Asian orchids only represented in the alpine garden by *B. striata* 30cm (12in) spikes of red-purple flowers in summer. Light shade and peaty soil. Suitable for the peat bed but can be also grown in the alpine house. Propagate by seed; self-sows.

Boykina see **Telesonix.**

Brachycome (Compositae) ○

From Australia and New Zealand. White or blue daisies; summer flowering; 15cm (6in) high. Sun and sharp drainage. Propagate by seed.

Briggsia (Gesneriaceae) ○▲

From Asia. Similar to ramondas with red or yellow flowers; summer flowering; 15cm (6in) high. Best grown in alpine house. Propagate by seed or division of offsets.

Bruckenthalia (Ericaceae) ○◑□☆

A one species genus (*B. spiculifolia*). Small shrub growing to 23cm (9in) with pink bell-shaped flowers, similar to heather; summer flowering. Propagate by division.

Bupleurum (Umbelliferae) ○☆

From around the northern hemisphere. Yellow-green flowers sometimes surrounded with green bracts; summer-flowering; up to 30cm (12in). Propagate by seed; some self-sow.

Calamintha (Labiatae) ○☆

Thyme-like subshrubs and herbs up to 23cm (9in). Pink or purple flowers and aromatic foliage; summer flowering. Sunny well-drained position; does well on walls. Propagate by cuttings or seed.

Calandrinia (Portulacaceae) ○▲

A relative of *Lewisia,* those grown coming mainly from South America. Succulent leaves and magenta, short-stemmed flowers; early summer flowering. Not long-lived. Sunny well-drained position, although best grown in alpine house. Propagate by seed. Not very easy for beginners.

Calceolaria (Scrophulariaceae) ◑
Mainly South American plants with a few suitable for the rock garden or alpine house. The flower has a slipper-like inflated bottom lip, mainly coloured yellow; summer flowering; up to 30cm (12in). Cool moist conditions in light shade; suitable for the peat garden. Propagate by division, cuttings or seed.

Callianthemum (Ranunculaceae) ○
Small, beautiful genus from Europe and Asia. White buttercup flowers sometimes tinged pink or lilac; spring flowering; up to 15cm (6in) high. For well-drained soil or, preferably, alpine house. Propagate by seed.

Calluna (Ericaceae) Ling ○☐☆
Single species genus (*C. vulgaris*) closely related to ericas. From North America, Europe and Asia. Colour of the bell-like flowers varies from white through pink to red. Propagate by cuttings.

Calochortus (Liliaceae) ○▲
Increasingly popular bulbous plants from North America and Mexico. Large range of colours. Some in flower in most seasons. Many tender, so they need a hot sunny position in well-drained soil or, preferably, bulb frame or alpine house treatment. Propagate by seed.

Caltha (Ranunculaceae) Marsh Marigold ○◑☆
World-wide distribution. Large buttercup, mainly yellow but also white; 30cm (12in) high; spring flowering. Likes moist, even boggy conditions. Suitable for a water feature or peat garden. Propagate by division or seed.

Campanula (Campanulaceae) Bellflower ○☆
Large and popular genus, characterised by its bell-like flowers. Rock garden forms up to 30cm (12in). Mainly blue but also white, pink and yellow; mainly summer flowering. They like sunny position in well-drained, moisture retentive soil. Some run around and can be invasive; others are monocarpic (die after flowering). Many suitable for troughs. Propagate by seed, division or cuttings.

Cardamine (Cruciferae) ◑☆
Large genus but only a few suitable for the rock garden. Pink or lilac, four-petalled flowers; spring flowering; up to 45cm (18in). They like light shade and moist soil conditions. Suitable for the peat garden. Propagate by seed or division.

Carduncellus (Compositae) ○
Small genus of thistles from the Mediterranean region, grown mainly for their decorative leaves. Blue flowers in early summer; up to 23cm (9in). Sunny well-drained position. Propagate by seed.

Carlina (Compositae) ○
Another genus of thistles from Europe and Mediterranean. Yellow or whitish 'everlasing' flowers, often stemless. Up to 30cm (12in). Sunny well-drained position on the rock or scree garden. Propagate by seed.

Cassiope (Ericaceae) ◑☐☐
Small lime-hating shrubs from the northern hemisphere. Often compact dome-shaped, covered in white or pink bell-shaped flowers; late spring flowering; up to

30cm (12in). Cool, acid, moist conditions, but best in part sun. Ideal for peat garden in sunny aspect. Propagate by cuttings.

Castilleja (Scrophulariaceae) ○▲
Tantalising genus from North America. Spectacular in flower with brightly coloured bracts, but, being semi-parasitic, they are very difficult to grow beyond the seedling stage. Planting several per pot or leaving a weed seedling as host sometimes helps until the plant is established. Propagate by seed.

Ceanothus (Rhamnaceae) ○
Genus of over 50 shrubs from North America, most too big for the rock garden but there are a couple of prostrate forms. Blue flowers appear in summer. Dwarf forms are relatively tender and need a warm sheltered spot in well-drained soil. Propagate by cuttings.

Celmisia (Compositae) ○
Large genus of plants mainly from New Zealand. Mostly grown for its hairy silvery-grey foliage, the daisy-like flowers are usually white, often with a yellow centre, appearing from early summer onwards. Some are up to 45cm (18in) or more but many are much smaller. Needs a warm, sunny position in a humus-rich soil. Many need overhead winter protection. Propagate by seed or cuttings.

Celsia (Scrophulariaceae) ○
The only one of this moderately sized genus suitable for the rock garden is the Greek *C. acasulis*. A 10cm (4in) plant with stemless yellow flowers similar to a verbascum, rising from a rosette of narrow toothed leaves. A hot sunny, well-drained position. Propagate by seed or root cuttings.

Centaurea (Compositae) Cornflower, Hardhead ○
Very large genus of which a few are grown by alpine gardeners. Most are too tall but there are several below 30cm (12in), with blue, purple, white or yellow cornflower-like flowers, in summer. Propagate by seed or division.

Centaurium (Gentianaceae) ○
About 50 world-wide species of which only one, *C. scilloides*, is generally grown. Resembles a pink *Gentiana verna*, up to 10cm (4in) tall; summer flowering. Sunny well-drained position. Propagate by seed.

Cerastium (Caryophyllaceae) ○
Sixty species from around the world, many of which are garden weeds. Some are suitable for the rock garden. Mat-forming plants, up to 7.5cm (3in), with large white flowers; summer flowering. Sunny position in any good soil. Propagate by seed or division.

Ceratostigma (Plumbaginaceae) ○☆
Small genus from Asia and Africa of which only one, *C. plumbaginoides*, is suitable for the rock garden. Large bright blue flowers on 30cm (12in) stems, with green leaves that take on autumn colours; autumn flowering. Gently running. Sunny well-drained position. Propagate by division or cuttings.

Chaenorrhinum (Scrophulariaceae) ○☆
Small genus similar to the linaria with toadflax-like flowers. Summer flowering with blue or purple flowers; short-lived. Sunny well-drained position. Propagate by seed; will self-sow.

Cheiranthus (Cruciferae) ○☆
Members of the wallflower family are split between this and *Erysimum*. This genus contains most of the larger garden plants including those for bedding purposes. Sunny position in well-drained soil. Short-lived. Propagate from cuttings or seed.

Chiastophyllum (Crassulaceae) ○◑☆
A monotypic genus from the Caucasus, *C. oppositifolium* (previously known as *Cotyledon oppositifolia*). Fleshy plant with arching stems of dangling yellow 'catkins' in summer; 15cm (6in) high. Sun or part shade in well-drained soil. Propagate by division or cuttings.

Chionodoxa (Liliaceae) Glory of the Snow ○
Small genus of small scilla-like bulbs. Pale to bright blue, starry flowers, usually with a white centre, in late winter and early spring; up to 15cm (6in). Sunny position and moist, humus-rich soil; dislikes a summer baking. Propagate by division or seed.

Chrysanthemum (Compositae) ○
Large genus of daisy-like flowers that is getting smaller as species are split off into *Agyranthemum, Leucanthemella, Leucanthemum, Tanacetum,* etc. Some dwarf forms up to 20–25cm (8–10in) worth growing in the rock garden. White, yellow, blue and purple flowers from summer onwards. Sunny position in any good, well-drained soil. Propagate by fresh seed or cuttings.

Cistus (Cistaceae) ○
Mediterrranean shrubs that are mainly too big for the rock garden. Some will fit into the larger garden as long as they have a hot position and very sharp drainage. Flowers are white or pink. Propagate by summer cuttings or from seed.

Claytonia (Portulacaceae) ○
Small genus of fleshy plants related to the lewisias with white, pink or red flowers, which appear in spring and summer. Sunny well-drained position. Propagate by seed or division; will self-sow.

Clematis (Ranunculaceae) ○
Large genus of climbing or shrubby plants. Until recently only *C. alpina* was considered by the alpine gardener, but recently several small New Zealand species have been received with great favour, particularly for the alpine house. They require a warm sunny position with a cool root-run. Propagate by seed or cuttings.

Clintonia (Liliaceae) ◑
North American and Asian woodland plants, grown for their white or pink flowers and their blue or black berries; up to 30cm (12in). Cool position in partial shade with a peaty soil; ideal for the peat garden. Propagate by division or seed.

Codonopsis (Campanulaceae) ○◑
Genus of increasing popularity from Asia. They are climbers or scramblers and need support. Bell-shaped flowers, usually of blue with coloured markings inside, best viewed from below; summer flowering. Well-drained soil in a sunny position, although some will take part-shade. Propagate by seed.

Colchicum (Liliaceae) ○☆
Confusingly called Autumn Crocuses, but crocuses they are not, although the general shape is the same. Flowers appear before the leaves. Mainly pink or light

purple, but also white and yellow species. Mostly autumn flowering, but there are also spring flowering species. Some will grow in grass, others need a sunny well-drained position or bulb-frame treatment. Propagate by division or seed. Common varieties easy for beginners.

Convallaria (Liliaceae) Lily-of-the-Valley ◑☆
Popular woodland species with white, fragrant bells; pink-flowered and variegated-leaved varieties sometimes seen; spring flowering. Runs with underground stolons; can be too invasive for the peat garden. Peaty, woodland soil, in shade. Propagate by division.

Convolvulus (Convolvulaceae) ○
Large genus in which there are some pernicious weeds. Some are better behaved and suitable for the rock garden. White, pink or blue trumpets apearing from late spring onwards. The better forms tend to be somewhat tender and need a hot sunny position with well-drained soil. Best to overwinter cuttings as insurance against loss. Propogate by cuttings.

Coprosma (Rubiaceae) ○
Shrubby plants from New Zealand and Australia of which *C. petriei* is the only species grown in the rock garden or alpine house in colder areas. Grown mainly for the translucent blue berries. 7.5cm (3in) high mat of branches. Warm, well-drained position. Propagate by cuttings.

Coptis (Ranunculaceae) ◑
Small genus, from North America and Japan, of woodland plants with white anemone-like flowers; spring flowering; up to 25cm (10in). Cool, shady conditions in leafy-woodland soil; ideal for the peat garden. Propagate by division.

Cornus (Cornaceae) ◑
Only two species of this genus of trees and shrubs are suitable for the rock garden: *CC. canadensis* and *suecia*. Both are spreading woodland plants with large white bracts surrounding the inconspicuous flowers. They are also grown for their autumn colour and berries. Shady conditions with leafy-woodland soil; good for the peat garden. Propagate by division or seed.

Corokia (Cornaceae) ○
Popular genus of small New Zealand shrubs with angular or contorted branches for which it is mainly grown. Yellow flowers in spring. Sunny well-drained position, tender in colder areas. Propagate by summer cuttings.

Cortusa (Primulaceae) ○
Small genus from Europe and Asia with close affinities to primulas. Drooping red or yellow flowers, held above round, hairy leaves, in late spring and early summer; up to 25cm (10in). Cool, shady woodland conditions; ideal for the peat garden. Propagate by seed.

Corydalis (Papaveraceae) ○◑
Increasingly popular large genus from the northern hemisphere. Although belonging to the poppy family they have small snapdragon-type flowers in a wide range of colours, and ferny foliage; up to 25cm (10in). Some have tuberous and others fibrous roots. Both are propagated by fresh seed. Requirements vary from sunny well-drained beds to peat beds. Most are hardy.

Cotoneaster (Rosaceae) ○☆
Genus of some 50 species of shrubs, a few of which are small enough for the rock garden. Most make tight prostrate mats up to 30cm (12in) high, that creep over the rocks. White flowers in spring followed by red berries and autumn tints in the leaves. Sunny position on any good soil. Propagate by cuttings.

Cotula (Compositae) ○☆
Large genus of mat-forming species from the southern hemisphere, particularly New Zealand. Ferny foliage topped with rayless flowers in a range of colours from yellow to deep red and purple. Good for ground cover but can become invasive. Propagate by division or seed.

Crassula (Crassulaceae) ○
Large genus of succulent plants from Africa of which a few are suitable for the alpine gardener. Pink or white flowers over fleshy leaves. Warm, sunny position in well-drained soil or alpine house. Propagate by cuttings.

Cremanthodium (Compositae) ○◑
Small genus from the Himalaya and China. Hanging heads of white or yellow flowers that do not seem to open fully; late summer flowering; up to 45cm (18in). Cool, moist conditions are preferred. Suitable for the rock garden. Propagate by seed.

Crepis (Compositae) ○☆
Large genus of dandelion- or hawkweed-like plants, some of which can be invasive. Colours vary from yellow to orange and pink; summer flowering. Up to 25cm (10in), but the dwarfer forms are best. Sunny position in well-drained soil. Propagate by seed.

Crocus (Iridaceae) ○☆
Large genus (80 species) of well-known and well-loved bulbs from Europe and Asia. Small goblets in a wide range of colours centred on white, yellow and blue; both spring and autumn flowering. In the main they prefer sunny position with well-drained soil; some prefer bulb-frame treatment. Propagate by seed or division. Some are easy for beginners.

Cyananthus (Campanulaceae) ○
Small genus from the Himalayas to China. Herbaceous perennials with blue flowers, in summer or autumn. Requires moisture and free drainage, so prefers sunny position with soil that has plenty of humus and grit. Propagate by cuttings and seed.

Cyclamen (Primulaceae) ◑☆
Small well-known genus of tubers from Europe, Near East and North Africa with pink or white flowers, some fragrant. They flower most months of the year except in the summer. About half will grow outside but the others need protection. Gritty compost with extra peat or leaf-mould in part shade is required, although they will grow in most soils. Propagate by seed; will self-sow. Hardy ones easy for beginners.

Cypripedium (Orchidaceae) Slipper Orchid ◑
About 50 species from the northern hemisphere some of which are suitable for the rock garden or alpine house. Delightful orchids with swollen pouches like slippers. Flowers in early summer. Grown in gritty peat in part shade; ideal for peat garden. Propagate by division.

Cytisus (Leguminosae) ○☆
Shrubby genus with a few suitable for the rock garden. Flowers are typically pea-like and usually yellow; summer flowering. Some of the dwarfer forms grow up to 60cm (2ft) high. Sunny position in any soil as long as it is free-draining. Propagate by cuttings.

Daboecia (Ericaceae) St Dabeoc's Heath ○□
A two-species genus from Europe and the Azores. A shrubby heath up to 60cm (2ft) but smaller if kept trimmed, with rosy-purple flowers in early summer. Sunny position in well-drained, peaty soil, which must be lime-free. Propagate by cuttings.

Daphne (Thymelaeceae) ○☆
These are one of the glories of the alpine garden. Nearly all the shrubs in this genus are suitable for the rock garden or alpine house. The starry flowers are mainly pink, but there are some white and yellow forms; many are fragrant; winter to summer flowering; Can be short-lived. Sunny position in well-drained soil. Propagate by cuttings, seed or grafting. Some are easy for beginners.

Delphinium (Ranunculaceae) ○☆
As well as the familiar giants of the herbaceous border, there are a number of smaller species up to 45cm (18in) in height, with mainly blue flowers, although there are some with white, yellow or red. Generally they are short-lived. Sunny, well-drained positions are needed. Propagate by seed. Some are easy for beginners.

Dianthus (Caryophyllaceae) ○☆
One of the most popular of all genera. Varying from tight, dwarf cushions to loose plants 35cm (14in) high. Flowers, which are often fringed and sometimes fragrant, are red, pink or white. They prefer full sun and well-drained soil. Propagate by cuttings or seed.

Diascia (Scrophulariaceae) ○☆
Increasingly popular genus from South Africa, with some of the species small enough for the rock garden. Small open-mouthed, pink flowers on domes or sprawling growth. Several will come through most winters but it is always advisable to overwinter cuttings as a safeguard. Sunny position in well-drained soil. Propagate by cuttings.

Dicentra (Papaveraceae) Bleeding Heart ◑
Small genus containing a few species suitable for the rock garden. Ferny foliage and arching stems of dangling locket-like flowers in red, pink or white. Foliage dies back after flowering. Part shade with gritty, moisture retentive soil. Propagate by seed.

Digitalis (Scrophulariaceae) Foxgloves ○◑☆
Most are too tall for the rock garden but some can be grown in the larger areas. Spires of thimble-like flowers of purple, white, yellow and brown, in early summer. Full sun or part shade with well-drained soil. Propagate by seed.

Dimorphoteca (Compositae) ○
Genus of tender plants from South Africa of which a few are hardy and small enough for the rock garden. Flat, daisy-like flowers in white or purple that need sun

to open fully. Overwinter cuttings as a safeguard. Sunny position in well-drained soil. Propagate by cuttings.

Dionysia (Primulaceae) ○□▲
Genus of cushion plants mainly from Iran and Afghanistan. To grow these well is a test of the grower's skills. Tight cushions of up to 7.5cm (3in) high with yellow or pink, small, long-tubed flowers. Require alpine house conditions to exclude the winter wet. Propagate by cuttings or seed.

Dodecatheon (Primulaceae) Shooting Stars ◑
Genus from North America of plants with cyclamen-like flowers on long stalks and with reflexed petals; summer flowering; up to 30cm (12in). Most prefer part-shade and a peaty soil, but a few like a sunny position with a gritty soil. Propagate by seed.

Dornicum (Compositae) ○☆
Genus of bright yellow daisies, most of which are too large for the rock garden. Attractive spring-flowering plants. Sunny position in any good soil. Propagate by division.

Douglasia (Primulaceae) ○
Cushion-forming plants from North America and Siberia, with a close affinity to androsaces. Long tubular flowers in pink appear in spring and summer. Sunny well-drained position or in the alpine house. Propagate by seed or rooted cuttings.

Draba (Cruciferae) ○
Very large genus of plants of which a number are valuable as cushion plants in the garden and alpine house. Yellow or white flowers clustered often on long thin stems, held above the cushions, up to 10cm (4in). Sunny well-drained position or in the alpine house. Propagate by seed.

Dracocephalum (Labiatae) ○
Small genus from Europe and Asia. Some are small enough for the rock garden being up to 30cm (12in) high. Flowers in spikes, usually of blue or purple; summer flowering. Sunny position with any good soil. Propagate by seed, cuttings or division.

Drosera (Droseraceae) Sundew ○
Small insectivorous plants with sticky leaves that trap insects. White flowers held on arching stems up to 10cm (4in) high. Needs a damp, even wet site; suitable for growing on pool margins. Propagate by seed.

Dryas (Rosaceae) ○☆
Prostrate subshrubs that carpet the ground, with glistening white flowers followed by fluffy seed heads; 10cm (4in) high; early summer flowering. Sunny position in well-drained soil. Propagate by seed.

Edraianthus (Campanulaceae) ○
Small genus mainly from Europe. Similar to the wahlenbergias except they have clustered instead of solitary purple flowers, usually bell-shaped. Summer flowering; up to 7.5cm (3in). Sunny well-drained position. Propagate by seed or cuttings.

Empetrum (Empetraceae) Crowberry ○□
Small genus of ten species of which only one, *E. nigrum,* is normally grown. It has pink bell-shaped flowers followed by black berries on a mat-forming plant up to

15cm (6in) high; summer flowering. Sunny position with moist peaty, lime-free soil. Propagate by cuttings.

Epigaea (Ericaceae) ◑☐
A three-species genus of low creeping plants with pink or white flowers; spring flowering. Needs shady situation with woodland soil (no lime). Ideal for a shaded peat bed. Propagate by cuttings.

Epilobium (Onagraceae) Willow Herb ○☆
Although many are weeds there are a few of the genus that are suitable for the rock garden. Pink or white flowers on plants of up to 20cm (8in); summer flowering. Sunny site in any good soil. Propagate by cuttings or seed.

Epimedium (Berberidaceae) ◑☆
Large woodland genus from Europe and Asia. Particularly valuable for their young leaves and the graceful arching stems of yellow, white, red or purple flowers; spring and summer flowering; up to 30cm (12in). Likes shady woodland conditions; ideal for the peat bed. Propagate by division and seed.

Epipactis (Orchidaceae) Hellborine ◑
Genus of 24 orchids, most of which are suitable for the peat garden. Summer flowering with mixed colours of green, purple and yellow flowers; up to 30cm (12in). Prefers a moist cool soil. Propagate by division.

Eranthis (Ranunculaceae) Winter Aconite ◑☆
A harbinger of spring, this genus has mainly yellow flowers surrounded by a ruff of leaves; 7.5cm (3in) high. Dies back after flowering. Prefers woodland soil that has summer shade. Suitable for the peat bed. Propagate by seed or division.

Erica (Ericaceae) Heather ○☐☆
Very large genus with many suitable species and cultivars for the garden. Pink or white flowers at different times of the year; many different colours of foliage. Sunny position with a free-draining, lime-free soil. Not really suitable for the rock garden but best grown amidst dwarf rhododendrons and other shrubs. Propagate by cuttings.

Erigeron (Compositae) ○☆
Large genus with quite a number dwarf enough for the rock garden. Daisies of blue, purple, white and yellow, flowering during spring and summer; up to 25cm (10in). Sunny position with any well-drained soil. Propagate by division or seed.

Erinacea (Leguminosae) ○
Genus with only one shrubby species, namely *E. anthyllis*. Forms a spiny hummock with lilac, pea-like flowers held amongst the tips of the spines; up to 30cm (12in). Hot, sunny spot with well-drained soil or for the alpine house. Propagate by cuttings.

Erinus (Scrophulariaceae) ○☆
Small genus of which one from Europe, *E. alpinus*, is suitable for the rock garden. Tufted plant with masses of pink or white flowers in summer; 7.5cm (3in) high. Not long-lived. Full sun in well-drained position. Suitable for crevices and walls. Propagate by seed.

Erigonum (Polygonaceae) ○
Large genus, from western North America, of perennial herbs and subshrubs, some cushion-forming. Flowers are mainly yellow but there are white- and pink-flowered species. Usually short-lived. Needs hot dry conditions, either in the rock garden or alpine house. Propagate by seed.

Eritrichium (Boraginaceae) ○▲
Notoriously difficult but very desirable genus, particularly in the species *E. nanum* with its bright blue flowers set off against a tight grey cushion; summer flowering. Needs alpine house treatment to keep it dry; do not overwater. Propagate by seed.

Erodium (Geraniaceae) ○☆
Small genus with several valuable plants for the rock garden. Flowers generally pink or white except for one yellow species; summer flowering, up to 20cm (8in). Sunny position in well-drained soil. Propagate by seed.

Eryngium (Umbelliferae) Sea Holly ○
Most too big except for the larger rock garden. Prickly, globular flower heads in blue or green; summer flowering. Tap-rooted, so difficult to move. Sunny position in deep well-drained soil. Propagate by seed or root cuttings.

Erysimum (Cruciferae) ○☆
Along with *Cheiranthus,* this constitutes the Wallflowers. Most of the species are usually listed under this genus. Flowers are mainly yellow; summer flowering. They like a sunny, well-drained position, making them suitable for crevices and walls. Short-lived, but they come readily from seed and cuttings.

Erythronium (Liliaceae) ◑☆
Genus of dwarf bulbs, mainly from North America, bearing nodding flowers with recurved petals of yellow or pink. Leaves sometimes marbled; spring-flowering; up to 30cm (12in). Prefers part shade in a woodland soil; perfect for the peat bed. Propagate by seed.

Euphorbia (Euphorbiaceae) ○◑☆
Enormous genus of over 2,000 species of which just a few are suitable for the rock garden. Their attraction is in the shape of the plant and the green bracts, the flowers being inconspicuous. Some are woodlanders and are suitable for the peat garden, others like a hot, dry situation. Propagate by seed, cuttings or division.

Euryops (Compositae) ○
Quite a large South African genus of which only one, *E. acraeus,* is generally grown in the rock garden. It is a small silver-leaved shrub with bright yellow flowers in early summer; up to 25cm (10in). Must have a sunny position with well-drained soil. Propagate by cuttings.

Festuca (Gramineae) ○☆
One of the few grasses that can be safely recommended for the rock garden. It makes clumps or tufts up to 30cm (12in) high. Sunny position in any good soil. Propagate by division.

Fragaria (Rosaceae) Wild Strawberry ○☆
Often seen on the mountainside but a bit of a risk in the rock garden as they are invasive. However, they are suitable for an alpine lawn or a sunny bank. Sunny position in any good soil. Propagate by runners.

Frankenia (Frankeniaceae) Sea Heath ○
Small genus of plants that resemble heather and grow near the sea. Mat-forming perennial herbs and subshrubs around the northern hemisphere. Pink or white flowers appear in summer; up to 10cm (4in). Sunny, well-drained position. Propagate by division or cuttings.

Fritillaria (Liliaceae) ○◑☆
Large genus of bulbs from around the northern hemisphere. Pendent flowers in a variety of yellow, brown, green and purple, often striped or chequered. In flower from early spring to summer; up to 60cm (24in). Majority like sunny, well-drained position, but some prefer more moist conditions in partial shade. Most grow well in the bulb frame or in pots. Propagate by seed. Some easy for the beginner.

Fuchsia (Onagraceae) ○
Not a genus normally associated with alpines, but there is one, *F. procumbens,* that is frequently grown. Curious flower with no petals and reflexed sepals, but it is for the berries that it is mainly grown. Summer flowering. Prostrate. Not fully hardy, so should be grown in the alpine house. Propagate by cuttings.

Gagea (Liliaceae) ○
Another large genus of bulbs, many of which are difficult to tell apart. Starry, yellow flowers of no more than 10cm (4in) in height; spring and summer flowering. Sunny position in peaty but well-drained soil. Propagate by seed or division.

Galanthus (Amaryllidaceae) Snowdrop ◑☆
Much loved genus of pendent white flowers from Europe and Asia, consisting of about 20 species and many cultivars and hybrids. Winter and spring flowering; up to 25cm (10in). Likes a partially shaded position in gritty-peaty soil. Propagate by division.

Gaultheria (Ericaceae) ◑□☆
Large genus of shrubs from around the world of which there are several low-growing species for the rock garden. Pink or white pendent flowers; summer flowering; up to 30cm (12in). Shady position in peaty soil; lime-hater. Suitable for the peat bed. Propagate by cuttings.

Genista (Leguminosae) ○☆
Large genus of shrubs with a few dwarf forms suitable for the rock garden. The yellow flowers are pea-like and appear in the summer; up to 30cm (12in). Sunny position in well-drained soil. Propagate by cuttings or seed.

Gentiana (Gentianaceae) ○◑☆
Large genus of wonderful, mainly blue flowers, but also containing, white and yellow species, flowering in the spring or autumn. European and New Zealand species prefer moisture retentive gritty soil in full sun; Asiatic species peaty soil in part shade. Propagate by division, cuttings or seed. Some easy for beginners.

Geranium (Geraniaceae) Cranesbill ○◑☆
Very large genus of plants from around the world, many of which are suitable for the rock garden. Flowers are mainly pink and purple; up to 30cm (12in). Sunny well-drained position; a few will stand partial shade. Propagate by seed, division or cuttings.

Geum (Rosaceae) ○☆
Quite a big genus of plants from around the world of which a few are suitable for rock gardens. Yellow, orange or red flowers on stems up to 30cm (12in) high; spring and summer flowering. Sunny position in any good soil. Propagate by division or seed.

Gladiolus (Iridaceae) ○
Large genus of which only one (*G. alatus*) is suitable for the rock garden. Yellow flowers up to 30cm (12in) high. Sunny position in well-drained soil. Propagate by division.

Glaucidium (Podophyllaceae) ◑
Single species genus (*G. palmatum*). Woodland plant from Japan with pinky-mauve or white flowers; up to 45cm (18in). Shady woodland conditions; ideal for the peat garden. Propagate by seed or division.

Globularia (Globulariaceae) ○
Genus from Europe and Asia, some of which are suitable for the rock garden. Round heads of blue flowers up to 30cm (12in); summer flowering. Sunny well-drained position. Propagate by seed.

Gypsophila (Caryophyllaceae) ○
Large genus of plants, mainly from Europe, of which a few are suitable for the rock garden, particularly those that are cushion- or mat-forming. White or pink flowers; up to 15cm (6in). Sunny well-drained position. Propagate by seed or cuttings.

Haberlea (Gesneriaceae) ◑
Small genus of two species from south-east Europe. Lilac-coloured flowers on arching stems; spring flowering; up to 15cm (6in). Shady, moist position. Suitable for a peat wall in the peat bed or in crevices on the north side of walls or rock gardens. Propagate by seed or division.

Hacquetia (Umbelliferae) ◑
Single species genus (*H. epipactis*) from Europe. Curious plant that flowers as it emerges from the soil in spring. Small yellow flowers surrounded by a collar of leafy bracts; 10cm (4in) high. Shady position in leafy, well-drained soil. Propagate by seed.

Hebe (Scrophulariaceae) ○◑☆
Large genus of shrubby veronicas from New Zealand, a few of which are suitable for the rock garden; some grown for their foliage effect. White or lilac flowers; summer flowering; up to 45cm (18in). May be tender in colder areas. Propagate by cuttings.

Helianthemum (Cistaceae) Rock Rose ○
Sun-loving plants from mainly around the Mediterranean. White, yellow, orange, red and pink flowers on small flopping shrubs; up to 20cm (8in). Sunny well-drained position. Propagate by cuttings or seed.

Helichrysum (Compositae) Everlasting Flower ○
Very large genus with just a handful suitable for the rock garden, mainly coming from South Africa and New Zealand. Most grown for their silvery foliage, the flowers being of little consequence; up to 30cm (12in). Hot, sunny, position in well-

drained soil. Many are better suited to the alpine house. Propagate by cuttings or seed.

Helleborus (Ranunculaceae) ◑☆
Genus of mainly European plants that are generally too large for the rock garden, yet are grown by most rock gardeners. Flowers of green, yellow, white or purple; spring flowering; up to 45cm (18in). Shady, gritty-peat conditions; ideal for the peat garden.

Hepatica (Ranunculaceae) ◑
This small genus is one of the delights of spring with its blue, pink, red or white flowers and three-lobed leaves; up to 7.5cm (3in). Prefers shady position in gritty-peaty soil. Ideal for the north side of a rock garden or peat bed. Propagate by seed or division.

Heuchera (Saxifragaceae) ○
Genus from North America with a few small species for the rock garden. Spikes of white or cream flowers in summer; up to 25cm (10in). Sunny well-drained position. Propagate by seed or division.

Hierachium (Compositae) Hawkweed ○
An enormous family, over 5,000 some claim, most too weedy for the rock garden. Mainly yellow-flowered with dandelion-like heads; up to 25cm (10in). Sunny position in any soil. Propagate by seed.

Horminum (Labiatae) ○
Single species genus (*H. pyrenaicum*), from Europe. Stems of violet-blue flowers in summer; up to 23cm (9in). Open, well-drained position. Propagate by seed or division.

Hosta (Liliaceae) ◑☆
A large genus of growing popularity. A number of smaller ones suitable for the peat garden. Grown mainly for their foliage but they also have attractive arching stems of white or pale blue flowers. Summer flowering; up to 25cm (10in). Prefer part shade and moist growing conditions; ideal for the peat garden. Propagate by division.

Houstonia (Rubiaceae) ◑☆
North American genus of which only one, *H. caerulea*, is generally grown. Mat-forming with pale blue flowers; summer flowering; 7.5cm (3in) high. Shady moist situation; good for the peat bed. Propagate by division.

Hutchinsia (Cruciferae) ○
This is a single species genus (*H. alpina*) from Europe. Low tufted plants with masses of white flowers in summer; 7.5cm (3in) high. Sunny well-drained position. Propagate by seed; self-sows.

Hyacinthus (Liliaceae) ○
Bulb best known in its blousy house-plant form, but there are some good species for the rock garden. Spikes of blue and white flowers, some sweetly scented; 20cm (8in) high; spring flowering. Sunny well-drained position. Propagate by seed or division.

Hylomecon (Papaveraceae) ◐
One species genus (*H. japonicum*) from Japan. Woodlander with rich yellow flowers; spring flowering; 30cm (12in) high. Shady woodland conditions; ideal for the peat bed. Propagate by seed.

Hypericum (Hypericaceae) ○☆
Large genus of shrubs with a number suitable for the rock garden. Yellow flowers with a prominent boss of stamens; summer flowering; up to 30cm (12in). Sunny well-drained position. Propagate by cuttings.

Hypsela (Campanulaceae) ◐
Small genus of creeping plants from the southern hemisphere. Pink flowers with crimson markings; summer flowering. Part shade, moist conditions. Suitable for the peat garden but can be invasive. Propagate by division.

Iberis (Cruciferae) Candytuft ○☆
Genus from Europe and Asia of tufted plants with white and mauve flowers; spring and summer flowering; up to 25cm (10in). Sunny well-drained position. Propagate by seed and cuttings.

Incarvillea (Bignoniaceae) ○
Small genus from China. Deep pink trumpets appear in summer; up to 45cm (18in). Sunny position in moisture retentive but well-drained soil. Propagate by seed.

Inula (Compositae) ○☆
Large genus of yellow daisies of which a few are small enough for the rock garden. Spring and summer flowering, up to 30cm (12in). Sunny, not too rich, well-drained soil. Propagate by division, seed or cuttings.

Ipheion (Amaryllidaceae) ○
Small genus of dwarf South American bulbs with blue or yellow flowers; spring flowering; up to 10cm (4in). Sunny position in well-drained soil. Suitable for the rock garden, bulb frame or alpine house. Propagate by division and seed.

Iris (Iridaceae) ○☆
Large genus of familiar garden plants with a wide range of colours. Many are small enough for the rock garden, bulb frame and alpine house. Winter, spring and summer flowering; up to 45cm (18in). Outside most require a sunny position, but some need well-drained soil while others need moist, peaty soil, often by water. Propagate by division and seed.

Isopyrum (Ranunculaceae) ◐
Small genus from North America with one species in general cultivation, *I. thalictroides*. Delicate woodland plant with white flowers; spring flowering; up to 15cm (6in). Shady woodland conditions; ideal for the peat garden. Propagate by seed or division.

Jankaea (Gesneriaceae) ◐▲
Single species genus (*J. heldreichii*) from Greece. A difficult plant with silvery leaves and blue flowers; spring flowering; 7.5cm (3in) high. Shady, well-drained soil in a crevice, but best in the alpine house. Propagate by leaf cuttings.

Jasione (Campanulaceae) ○
Small genus of herbaceous perennials, typified by their rounded heads of blue flowers; summer flowering; up to 25cm (10in). Sunny position in any good soil. Propagate by seed or division.

Jeffersonia (Berberidaceae) ◑
A choice genus of only two species from North America and Manchuria. White and purple flowers in spring; up to 20cm (8in). Woodlanders needing shade and gritty-peaty soil; ideal for the peat bed. Propagate by seed. Now officially called *Plagiorhegma*, but still mainly known as *Jeffersonia*.

Kalmia (Ericaceae) ◑▢▢
Small shrubby genus from North America, of which only a couple are suitable for the rock garden. Pink, widely flared flowers in late spring and early summer; up to 60cm (24in). For a partly shaded position in a peaty soil; lime-hater; ideal for the rock garden. Propagate by cuttings.

Kalmiopsis (Ericaceae) ◑▢▢
One species genus (*K. leachiana*) from North America. Small evergeen shrub with dark pink flowers; spring flowering; 30cm (12in) high. Shady peaty soil; lime-hater; ideal for the peat bed or suitable for the alpine house. Propagate by cuttings.

Kelseya (Rosaceae) ○
One species genus (*K. uniflora*) from North America. Cushion plant with tiny white flowers, grown for its minute silvery foliage. Late spring flowering; 1.25cm (½in) high. Sunny well-drained position in a trough or best in alpine house. Propagate by division, cuttings or seed.

Lapeirousia (Iridaceae) ○
Small genus of bulbs from South Africa. The one usually grown in rock gardens is *L. laxa* with narrow leaves and red flowers; summer flowering; 30cm (12in) high. Sunny well-drained position. Tender in some areas. Propagate by seed.

Lathyrus (Leguminosae) ○☆
Large genus of vigorous climbers and herbaceous perennials. A few are suitable for the rock garden. Red, purple and orange pea-like flowers, spring and summer flowering; up to 45cm (18in). Sunny well-drained position, although some will take part shade. Propagate by seed.

Ledum (Ericacae) ◑▢▢
Small genus of shrubs from North America with white or pink flowers. Late spring flowering; up to 45cm (18in). Cool, part shady conditions with a gritty-peaty soil; lime-hater. Suitable for the peat garden. Propagate by cuttings.

Leontopodium (Compositae) Edelweiss ○
Silver-leaved plants from Europe and Asia. Small flowers enclosed in white woolly bracts; summer flowering; up to 20cm (8in). Sunny well-drained position. Propagate by seed.

Leptospermum (Myrtaceae) ○▢▢
Genus of shrubs mainly from New Zealand and Australia. Mainly too tender or too large for the rock garden, but a few species and cultivars are suitable. Small red, pink or white flowers cover the plant in summer. Hot sunny position with good drainage; lime-hater. Propagate by cuttings.

Leucanthemum (Compositae) ○☆
Small genus consisting of refugees from the genus *Chrysanthemum*. White daisies some with a long flowering season; spring and summer flowering; up to 15cm (6in). Sunny well-drained site. Propagate by cuttings.

Leucogenes (Compositae) ○
Two species genus from New Zealand which consists of the equivalent to the European Edelweiss. Grown for its silvery appearance; up to 20cm (8in). A plant for the alpine house, but can be grown in a sunny well-drained position. Propagate by seed.

Leucojum (Amaryllidaceae) Snowflake ○◗
Small genus of bulbs from Europe and North Africa, closely related to the Snowdrops. White, pendulous flowers; spring and autumn flowering; up to 30cm (12in). Sunny or part shade in gritty-peat soil. Smaller species best grown in alpine house or bulb frame. Propagate by seed or division.

Lewisia (Portulacaceae) ○
Very popular genus of plants from North America. The flowers, particularly of some of the hybrids, are brightly coloured, in red, orange, white, pink and apricot. Summer flowering; up to 15cm (6in). Best grown in the alpine house or frames, but will grow in a warm, sunny vertical crevice. Propagate by seed.

Lilium (Liliaceae) ○◗
Well-known genus of plants from around the northern hemisphere. A few are small enough to grow in the rock garden. Wide variety of colours available; summer flowering; up to 45cm (18in). Prefers a gritty-peaty soil in full sun or partial shade. Propagate by seed or division.

Limonium (Plumbaginaceae) Statice ○
Large genus (300 species) of which a few species are suitable for alpine use. Sprays of papery flowers in white, pink, blue or purple; summer flowering; up to 45cm (18in). Sunny position in any good soil. Propagate by seed.

Linaria (Scrophulariaceae) Toadflax ○☆
Large genus particularly from the Mediterranean region. Snapdragon-type flowers in a wide range of colours; summer flowering; up to 30cm (12in). Sunny position in well-drained soil. Some can be invasive; some need alpine house protection. Propagate by seed or division. Most easy for beginners.

Linnaea (Caprifoliaceae) ◗☆
One species genus (*L. borealis*) from around the northern hemisphere. Carpet-former with little pink bell-shaped flowers; summer flowering; 7.5cm (3in) high. Cool woodland conditions. Suitable for the peat bed, but may become invasive. Propagate by cuttings or division.

Linum (Linaceae) Flax ○☆
Large genus coming particularly from the Mediterranean region. Tufted plants with blue, white, yellow and pink flowers; summer flowering; up to 30cm (12in). Not long-lived. Sunny well-drained position. Propagate by seed.

Lithodora (Boraginaceae) ○☆
Small genus of shrubby plants, mainly from Europe. Blue-flowered, from spring into autumn; up to 20cm (8in). Sunny well-drained position. Propagate by cuttings.

Lithophragma (Saxifragaceae) ◑
Small genus from western North America of which one, *L. parviflorum*, is in general cultivation. White or pink starry flowers on thin stems; late spring flowering; up to 15cm (6in). Shady woodland conditions; suitable for the peat garden. Propagate by seed or division.

Loiseleuria (Ericaceae) ○☐
One species genus (*L. procumbens*) with circumpolar distribution. Dwarf, prostrate, creeping azalea with pink, bell-shaped flowers; summer flowering. Open situation with gritty-peaty soil; lime-hater. Shy flowering in cultivation. Propagate by cuttings.

Lubinus (Leguminosae) ○
This well-known garden plant has several smaller relations that are suitable for the rock garden, mainly coming from North America. Spikes of pea flowers, mostly in blue; up to 60cm (24in). Warm sunny position with well-drained soil; some prefer alpine house treatment. Propagate by seed.

Lychnis (Caryophyllaceae) ○☆
Most of this genus are too large for the rock garden, but there are a few suitable species. Pink or red flowers; spring and summer flowering; up to 30cm (12in). Sunny position with any good soil. Propagate by seed or cuttings.

Lysimachia (Primulaceae) ○
Large genus of plants with a few small enough for the rock garden. Flowers are red or yellow, appearing in summer; up to 30cm (12in). Sunny position in any good soil. Propagate by division.

Matthiola (Cruciferae) ○
Large genus with a few species for the rock garden. Flowers usually purple and often scented; spring flowering; up to 20cm (8in). Short-lived. Sunny well-drained position. Some can be invasive. Propagate by seed or division.

Mazus (Scrophulariaceae) ○
Low-growing herbs, related to the mimulus. White, yellow and blue flowers in the spring and early summer; up to 7.5cm (3in). Sunny well-drained position. Propagate by seed or cuttings.

Meconopsis (Papaveraceae) ◑
Splendid genus of blue poppies that also includes species with yellow, red and purple flowers, mainly from Asia. Summer flowering; up to 1m (36in). Needs cool, moist position and does particularly well in the peat garden. Propagate by seed.

Mentha (Labiatae) Mint ◑
Generally this genus is too rampant for the rock garden, but the tiny, prostrate *M. requenii* can be allowed into the peat bed, but even this can be invasive. Cool moist, peaty position. Propagate by division.

Merendera (Liliaceae) ○
Bulbous plant very similar to the colchicums. Small plants with white or pink flowers, best suited to the bulb frame; spring or autumn flowering. Propagate by seed or division.

Mertensia (Boraginaceae) ◑
Quite a large genus of plants of which a number are suitable for the rock garden; some are mat-forming. Glaucous blue foliage and blue, forget-me-not flowers are characteristic of the plants; spring and summer flowering; up to 45cm (18in). Cool position in gritty-peaty soil. Suitable for the peat garden or shady side of rock garden. Propagate by seed or division.

Micromeria (Labiatae) ○
Large genus of aromatic shrubs and herbs, with some suited to the rock garden. Small thyme-like flowers in pink or purple; summer flowering; up to 15cm (6in). Beloved by cats. Needs warm, sunny position in well-drained soil. Tender in some areas. Propagate by cuttings or seed.

Mimulus (Scrophulariaceae) Musk ○☆
Large family with many suitable for the peat bed. Yellow or red flowers from summer onwards; up to 30cm (12in). Sunny position with cool root-run in gritty peat. Propagate by cuttings or seed.

Minuartia (Caryophyllaceae) ○☆
Large genus of cushion-forming or creeping plants. Minute white flowers in summer; up to 15cm (6in). Sunny well-drained position; many suitable for trough culture. Propagate by seed or division.

Mitella (Saxifragaceae) ◑
Small woodland genus mainly from North America. White or greenish flowers on spreading or tufted plants; spring flowering; up to 30cm (12in). Cool woodland conditions. Suitable for the peat bed. Propagate by division or seed; self-sows.

Moltkia (Boraginaceae) ○
Small genus of which the subshrubs, related to the lithodoras, are of interest. Blue flowers appear in summer; up to 20cm (8in). Sunny position wtih well-drained soil. Propagate by cuttings.

Monardella (Labiatae) ○
Genus of 20 species from western North America; a small version of the related monardas. Aromatic foliage and pink, red, purple or yellow flowers; summer flowering; up to 20cm (8in). Warm sunny position in very well-drained soil. May be tender in many areas and require alpine house treatment. Propagate by seed.

Morisia (Cruciferae) ○
One species genus (*M. monanthos*) from Sardinia and Corsica. Bright yellow flowers in spring rising from a tufted rosette of shiny, dark green leaves; 5cm (2in) high. Sunny well-drained position. Particularly good for troughs and the alpine house. Propagate by seed or root cuttings.

Muscaria (Liliaceae) Grape Hyacinth ○☆
Large genus of dwarf bulbs, mainly from the Mediterranean region and the Near East. Flowers mainly blue and appearing in the spring; up to 25cm (10in). Sunny position in well-drained soil. Propagate by division or seed. Some species are invasive.

Myosotis (Boraginaceae) Forget-me-not ○
Medium-sized genus from around the world. Mainly blue flowers, but also white

and even yellow; spring and summer flowering; up to 20cm (8in). Sunny position in gritty-peaty soil. Propagate by seed.

Narcissus (Amaryllidaceae) ○☆
Well-known genus of dwarf bulbs. Yellow, trumpeted flowers produced in the spring; up to 25cm (10in). Sunny well-drained spot although many prefer alpine house or bulb frame culture. Propagate by division or from seed. Some easy for beginners.

Nerine (Amaryllidaceae) ○
Bulbs from South Africa which are generally too large for the rock garden. *N. filifolia,* however, is a good pink-flowered plant for the bulb frame or alpine house. Autumn flowering; 20cm (8in). Propagate by seed or division.

Nierembergia (Solanaceae) ○
Genus of 35 plants mainly from South America; two generally grown in the rock garden. Campanula-like flowers in white or mauve; summer flowering; up to 15cm (8in) high, some mat-forming. Sunny well-drained position. Propagate by division or seed.

Nomocharis (Liliaceae) ◑
Genus of bulbs from the Himalaya to China. Delightful pendent, pink, white and yellow flowers like saucer-shaped lilies; summer flowering; up to 75cm (30in). Cool position with gritty-peaty soil. Propagate by seed.

Oenothera (Onagraceae) Evening Primrose ○☆
Large genus from North America with a few small enough for the rock garden. Yellow or white flowers mainly opening towards the evening; summer flowering; up to 25cm (10in). Warm sunny position with well-drained soil. Not long-lived. Propagate by seed. Some easy for beginners.

Omphalodes (Boraginaceae) ○◑
Delightful genus of blue or white forget-me-not flowers from Europe and Asia. Spring and summer flowering; up to 25cm (10in). *OO. cappadocica* and *verna* need shady woodland conditions; *OO. linifolia* (annual) and *luciliae* need sunny well-drained position, the latter preferring alpine house treatment. Propagate by division or seed.

Omphalogramma (Primulaceae) ◑▲
Small genus from Tibet and China related to the primulas. Purple flowers; spring and summer flowering; up to 20cm (8in). Cool, shady position with peaty soil. Suitable for peat garden. Propagate by seed.

Ononis (Leguminosae) Rest Harrow ○
Medium-sized genus with plants from Europe into central Asia. Shrubs and perennial herbs with pea-like flowers in pink or yellow; summer flowering; up to 60cm (24in). Sunny well-drained position. Propagate by seed or cuttings.

Onosma (Boraginaceae) ○
Intriguing genus of bristly plants with pendent tubular flowers of white, pink, yellow or blue; summer flowering; up to 25cm (10in). Sunny well-drained position. Propagate by seed.

Ophrys (Orchidaceae) ○▲
Genus of difficult-to-grow orchids that mimic insects. Spring and summer flowering; up to 25cm (10in). Best grown in the alpine house. Propagate by division. Very difficult.

Orchis (Orchidaceae) ○◑▲
Another genus of terrestrial orchids, easier to grow than the previous genus. Mainly purple and pink in colour; spring and summer flowering; up to 30cm (12in). Sunny or part shady conditions in any good soil. Propagate by division.

Origanum (Labiatae) Marjoram ○☆
Small genus of aromatic herbs from Europe and west Asia. Pink or purple flowers on subshrubs; summer flowering; 20cm (8in) high. Sunny well-drained position. Propagate by cuttings, division or seed. Most easy for beginners.

Ornithogalum (Liliaceae) ○☆
Large genus of mainly dwarf bulbs. White star-like flowers in spring; up to 15cm (6in). Sunny well-drained position. Propagate by division or seed; some multiply rather rapidly.

Ourisia (Scrophulariaceae) ◑
About 25 species from the southern hemisphere, several of which are good for the peat garden or alpine house. Mat-forming with pink, white or red flowers; spring or summer flowering; up to 30cm (12in). Cool, shady, moist position with peaty soil. Ideal for the peat bed.

Oxalis (Oxalidaceae) ○☆
Very large genus of 800 species from around the world. Some can become garden pests. Funnel-shaped flowers of pink, yellow, white or mauve; summer flowering; up to 25cm (10in). Sunny well-drained position. Propagate by seed or division; some are invasive.

Oxytropis (Leguminosae) ○
Large genus, from around the northern hemisphere, of 300 species of subshrubs and perennial herbs. Pea-like flowers of white, red, blue, mauve and purple; summer flowering; up to 25cm (10in). Sunny well-drained position. Propagate by seed.

Papaver (Papaveraceae) Poppy ○☆
Large, well-known genus with many species for the alpine garden. Fleeting, tissuey flowers of white, yellow, orange or red; summer flowering; up to 25cm (10in). Sunny well-drained position. Propagate by seed.

Paraquilegia (Ranunculaceae) ○
Small but very attractive genus, from Himalaya to China, of mauve flowers over delicate foliage. Spring flowering; up to 15cm (6in). Sunny well-drained position, preferably in a trough, tufa or alpine house. Propagate by seed.

Parnassia (Parnassiaceae) ○◑
Fifty species from around the northern hemisphere, with a few suitable for the alpine garden. Cool white flowers, often green-veined; summer flowering; up to 30cm (12in). Cool position in peaty soil; also suitable for sunny position in the peat bed. Propagate by seed.

Parochetus (Leguminosae) ○☆
Single species genus mainly from the Himalaya. Carpet-forming with bright blue pea-like flowers; summer and autumn flowering; 7.5cm (3in) high. Sunny well-drained position. Propagate by division. Can be invasive, but cut back by frosts.

Paronychia (Caryophyllaceae) ○☆
Fifty species from around the world, of which a few are suitable for the alpine garden. Small inconspicuous flowers with attractive bracts; carpet-forming; summer flowering; prostrate. Sunny well-drained position. Propagate by division.

Parrya (Cruciferae) ○
Small genus of dwarf wallflowers, with fragrant flowers of white, yellow, pink or purple. Early summer flowering; up to 20cm (8in). Sunny well-drained position. Propagate by cuttings or seed.

Pedicularis (Scrophulariaceae). ○▲
Very large genus (500 species) of semi-parasites that are not easy to grow. Flowers of wide range of colours; up to 30cm (12in). Sunny well-drained position. Propagate by seed.

Penstemon (Scrophulariaceae) ○☆
Very large genus mainly from western North America, of which quite a few are suitable for the rock garden. Mainly blue, purple and red flowers; summer flowering; up to 30cm (12in). Sunny well-drained position. Propagate by seed or cuttings. Some easy for beginners.

Perezia (Compositae) ○
Large genus from the Americas. Daisy-like flowers, some of which are blue; summer flowering; up to 30cm (12in). Sunny well-drained position. Propagate by seed.

Pernettya (Ericaceae) ○◑☐☆
Shrubby genus mainly from New Zealand, Tasmania and South America. White urn-shaped flowers, but mainly grown for their decorative berries; summer flowering. Sunny or part shady position, with gritty-peaty soil; lime-haters. Propagate by cuttings.

Philesia (Philesiaceae) ◑☐
Single species genus (*P. magellanica*) from Chile. Monocot shrub with red, tubular flowers appearing in summer; 30cm (12in) high. Peaty lime-free soil, in shady position. Propagate by cuttings or division. Takes a while to settle down.

Phlox (Polemoniaceae) ○◑☆
Large genus mainly from North America. There are many smaller species and cultivars suitable for the rock garden, often carpeters with round flowers in a wide range of colours; up to 20cm (8in). Generally like sunny, well-drained position, though some prefer cooler situation. Propagate by cuttings or seed.

Phuopsis (Rubiaceae) ○☆
One species genus (*P. stylosa*) from the Caucasus. Carpet-forming, aromatic plant with airy balls of pink flowers; summer flowering; 20cm (8in) high. Sunny well-drained position. Propagate by cuttings or division.

Phyllodoce (Ericaceae) ◑☐☆
Small genus of circumpolar shrubs. Pink or purple, urn-shaped flowers appear in spring and early summer; up to 25cm (10in). Cool peaty conditions; lime-hater. Ideal for the peat garden.

Physoplexus (Campanulaceae) ○
One species genus (*P. comosa*), formerly in *Phyteuma*. Very distinct flower head like a collection of tear-drops, shading from dark to light violet blue; 7.5cm (3in) high. Sunny well-drained position; best grown in a trough, tufa or alpine house. Propagate by seed.

Phyteuma (Campanulaceae) ○☆
Mainly from Europe. Dense, shaggy spikes or heads of blue flowers; summer flowering; up to 30cm (12in). Sunny well-drained position. Propagate by seed. Some easy for beginners.

Pinguicula (Lentibulariaceae) Butterwort ○◑
Forty-six species of insectivorous plants from around the world. Insects are captured on the sticky leaves. White, blue or purple flowers in early summer; up to 10cm (4in). Wet boggy conditions required. Propagate by leaf cuttings or division.

Plagiorhegma see ***Jeffersonia.***

Plantago (Plantaginaceae) Plantain ○☆
Surprisingly, there are a few of this genus that are suitable for the rock garden. It is usually the foliage that provides the attraction; up to 15cm (6in). Sunny well-drained position. Propagate by division or seed.

Platycodon (Campanulaceae) ○☆
One species genus from north-east Asia. Large purple flowers, inflated in bud; summer flowering; 30cm (12in) high. Sunny well-drained position. Propagate by seed or division.

Pleione (Orchidaceae) ◑
Increasingly popular genus from the Himalaya to China for the peat garden and alpine house. Short hooded flowers of purple, white or yellow; spring or autumn flowering; up to 7.5cm (3in). Cool, peaty soil. Best treated as alpine house plants. Propagate by division and seed.

Polemonium (Polemoniaceae) Jacob's Ladders ○☆
Genus of large perennial plants with a few smaller ones suitable for the rock garden. Funnel-shaped flowers in pink, mauve, yellow and white; summer flowering; up to 30cm (12in). Sunny well-drained position. Propagate by seed.

Polygala (Polygalaceae) Milkwort ○☆
Large genus, over 500 species, with world-wide distribution. Some are herbs; others shrubby. Several compact species are useful for the alpine garden. Small pea-like flowers in blue, white, yellow and purple; late spring and summer flowering; up to 15cm (6 in). Sunny well-drained position. Propagate by cuttings.

Polygonatum (Liliaceae) Solomon's Seal ◑☆
Genus of 50 species of herbaceous plants. Some are too tall for the alpine garden, but several of these gracious plants will find a place in the peat garden. White

tubular flowers hang from arching stems; spring flowering. Shade and cool peaty soil. Propagate by division.

Polygonum (Polygonaceae) ○☆
Large genus from around the world. Some of the smaller ones make good ground cover in the alpine garden. Spikes of pink, red or white flowers; summer and autumn flowering; up to 30cm (12in). Sunny conditions in any good soil. Propagate by division.

Potentilla (Rosaceae) Cinquefoil ○☆
Five hundred species of shrubby and herbaceous plants from around the world; large numbers are suitable for the alpine garden. Yellow, orange, red or white flowers; summer flowering; up to 60cm (24in). Sunny well-drained position. Propagate by cuttings, division or seed.

Pratia (Campanulaceae) ○☆
Creeping plants mainly from the southern hemisphere. Blue or white starry flowers from summer onwards. Prostrate. Gritty-peaty soil. Propagate by division. Many are invasive.

Primula ((Primulaceae) ○◖☆
Very large genus of well-loved plants for the rock garden and peat bed, from around the world. Flowers found in a large variety of colours; up to 45cm (18in). A wide variety of conditions and soils; many suitable for the peat bed. Some easy for beginners.

Prunella (Labiatae) Self-heal ○◖☆
Small genus of herbs from the northern hemisphere. Short spikes of pink or purple labiate flowers; summer flowering; up to 15cm (6in). Sunny or part-shaded position, in any good soil. Propagate by division.

Prunus (Rosaceae) ○☆
Enormous genus of trees and shrubs of which a few are small enough to be grown in the rock garden; some creeping. White or pink flowers in spring; up to 30cm (12in). Sunny well-drained position. Propagate by cuttings.

Ptilotrichum (Cruciferae) ○
Small genus related to *Alyssum*, but having white or pink flowers. Spring and summer flowering; up to 23cm (9in). Sunny well-drained position. Propagate by cuttings or seed.

Pulmonaria (Boraginaceae) Lungwort ◖☆
Small European genus that grows well in the peat garden. Bristly leaves and funnel-shaped flowers of red, pink, blue or white; spring flowering, 20cm (8in) high. Shady position with gritty-peaty soil. Propagate by division.

Pulsatilla (Ranunculaceae) ○☆
Small genus of very similar plants most of which are suitable for the rock garden. Flowers of purple, red, white or yellow; spring flowering; up to 30cm (12in). Sunny well-drained position. Propagate by seed or root cuttings.

Puschkinia (Liliaceae) ○☆
Small genus of dwarf bulbs. Pale blue flowers in spring; 12cm (5in) high. Sunny well-drained position. Propagate by division.

Pyrola (Pyrolaceae) Wintergreen ◑▲
Small genus of creeping woodland plants. Stems of white bell-shaped flowers; summer flowering; up to 25cm (10in). Cool, shady conditions in woodland soil. Suitable for the peat garden, but resents disturbance. Propagate by division.

Ramonda (Gesneriaceae) ◑
European genus of three species. Mauve flowers in spring or early summer; up to 15cm (6in). Crevices in north-facing rockwork with humus rich, well-drained soil. Propagate by seed or leaf cuttings.

Ranunculus (Ranunculaceae) ○☆
Very large genus from around the world. Many suitable for the rock garden. Mainly yellow or white flowering, in spring and summer; up to 30cm (12in). Sunny well-drained position, some preferring moister conditions. Propagate by seed or division. Some easy for beginners.

Raoulia (Compositae) ○
Genus from New Zealand and other parts of Australasia. Mat- or cushion-forming plants grown for their foliage effect; prostrate. Sunny well-drained position. Propagate by cuttings or seed.

Rhododendron (Ericaceae) ○◑▣☆
Very large genus of trees and shrubs of which a large number are suitable for the alpine garden. Flowers in a variety of colours in spring and early summer; up to 60cm (24in). Sunny or part shade with gritty-peaty soil; lime-haters. Propagate by cuttings or seed. Some easy for beginners.

Rhodohypoxis (Hypoxidaceae) ○
Small genus of dwarf bulbs from southern Africa. Red, pink or white flowers, from late spring onwards; up to 15cm (6in). Sunny position in moist gritty-peaty soil. Suitable for the peat bed but requires winter protection. Propagate by division and seed.

Romulea (Iridaceae) ○
Genus of dwarf bulbs of about 50 species, from the Mediterranean and southern Africa. Flowers similar to crocuses, mainly of violet colour; up to 15cm (6in). Sunny well-drained position; some need alpine house or bulb frame protection. Propagate by division or seed.

Roscoea (Zingiberaceae) ○
Small genus from the Himalaya to China, gaining in popularity. Hooded flowers of yellow or purple somewhat like large orchids; summer flowering; up to 30cm (12in). Sunny, humus-rich, well-drained position. Propagate by division or seed.

Rupicapnos (Papaveraceae) ○
Genus from around the Mediterranean and North Africa of corydalis-like, whitish flowers; summer flowering; up to 15cm (6in). Sunny well-drained position. Propagate by seed.

Sagina (Caryophyllaceae) Pearlwort ○☆
Some are pests but others are worthy rock garden plants. Cushion- or mat-forming with small white flowers in early summer; prostrate. Sunny well-drained position. Propagate by seed or division.

Salix (Salicaceae) Willow ○◐☆
Very large genus of 500 species of trees and shrubs, some of which are small enough for the rock garden. Catkins of yellow, white, purple and orange; spring flowering; up to 30cm (12in). Sunny or part shade in any good garden soil. Propagate by cuttings.

Sanguinaria (Papaveraceae) Bloodroot ◐□☆
Single species genus (*S. canadensis*) from North America. White flowers, particularly spectacular in its double form; 10cm (4in) high. Partial shade in woodland soil; ideal for a lime-free peat garden. Propagate by division.

Saponaria (Caryophyllaceae) Soapwort ○☆
Small genus from Europe and Asia, which has a few dwarf forms. Flowers are mainly pink; summer flowering; up to 10cm (4in). Sunny well-drained position. Propagate by cuttings or seed.

Sarcocapnos (Papaveraceae) ○
Small genus resembling *Rupicapnos*. Ferny foliage with yellowish flowers in early summer; 12cm (5in) high. Sunny well-drained position. Short-lived. Propagate by seed.

Satureja (Labiatae) ○☆
Aromatic herbs and dwarf shrubs. White, pink or mauve flowers; summer flowering; up to 30cm (12in). Sunny well-drained position. Propagate by cuttings.

Saussurea (Compositae) ○
Very large genus mainly from Asia of thistle-like plants, some of which seem to be covered in cotton wool. A few grown in the alpine garden. Summer flowering; up to 30cm (12in). Sunny well-drained position. Propagate by seed.

Saxifraga (Saxifragaceae) ○◐☆
Very large and important genus for the rock gardener. Flowers in yellow, white, pink and purple; spring and summer flowering; up to 30cm (12in). Sunny or part shady position in well-drained soil. Propagate by cuttings or seed. Some easy for beginners.

Scabiosa (Dipsaceae) ○☆
Large genus of plants, many of which are too tall for the rock garden. Lilac to purple flowers appear in the summer; up to 25cm (10in) high. Sunny well-drained position. Propagate by division or seed.

Scilla (Liliaceae) ○☆
Large genus of dwarf bulbs. Flowers blue to purple, in spring, summer or autumn; up to 30cm (12in). Sunny well-drained position. Propagate by seed or division.

Scoliopus (Liliaceae) ◐
Small genus of two species from North America with curious brownish-purple flowers; spring flowering; up to 7.5cm (3in). Cool, shady position in peaty soil. Ideal for the peat garden. Propagate by seed or division.

Scutellaria (Labiatae) Skull-cap ○☆
Large genus from throughout the world of which a few are suitable for the rock garden. Blue to purple and cream, labiate flowers; summer flowering; up to 25cm (10in). Sunny well-drained position. Propagate by cuttings or seed.

Sedum (Crassulaceae) Stonecrop ○☆
Very large genus of 600 species of fleshy, succulent-leaved plants, mainly from the northern hemisphere; many suitable for the rock garden. Flowers yellow, white, red or purple; spring, summer or autumn flowering; up to 30cm (12in). Sunny well-drained position. Propagate from cuttings or seed; some can be invasive.

Semiaquilegia (Ranunculaceae) ○
Small genus similar to the aquilegias except flowers have no spurs; white or purple; summer flowering; up to 45cm (18in). Sunny well-drained position. Propagate by seed.

Sempervivum (Crassulaceae) House-leek ○☆
Genus of 25 species and many hybrids and cultivars. Rosette-forming, fleshy-leaved plants with yellow, red or purple flowers; summer and autumn flowering; up to 20cm (8in). Sunny well-drained position. Propagate by offsets.

Senecio (Compositae). ○☆
Very large genus (up to 3,000 species according to some authorities) from around the world of daisy-like flowers, mainly yellow or white in colour; summer flowering; up to 30cm (12in). Sunny well-drained position. Propagate by seed, cuttings or division.

Serapias (Orchidaceae) ○▲
Beautiful genus of 10 species of European orchids. Mainly brownish-purple flowers; spring flowering; up to 30cm (12in). Sunny position with humus-rich, well-drained soil. Perhaps best grown in alpine house or bulb frame. Propagate by division.

Shortia (Diapensiaceae) ◐
Small genus from the Far East and North America. Funnel-shaped flowers in white or pink; spring and summer flowering; up to 20cm (8in). Cool, shady position in humus-rich soil. Ideal for the peat garden., Propagate by seed.

Silene (Caryophyllaceae) Campion ○◐☆
Large genus (500 species) from around the northern hemisphere; some cushion-forming. White, pink or red flowers; late spring and summer flowering; up to 30cm (12in). Sun or part shade in any good garden soil. Propagate by seed; some self-sow.

Sisyrinchium (Iridaceae) ○☆
Large genus of 100 species from the Americas. Flared, starry flowers are either blue, yellow or white; summer flowering; up to 30cm (12in). Sunny well-drained position. Propagate by seed or division; some may be invasive.

Soldanella (Primulaceae) ○◐
Delightful genus of fringed bell-like flowers from Europe; mauve in colour; spring flowering; up to 10cm (4in). Cool open position with a humus-rich soil. Suitable for the peat garden or in shady parts of the rock garden. Propagate by division or seed.

Solidago (Compositae) Goldenrod ○☆
Large genus mainly from North America, with a few small enough for the rock garden. Yellow-flowered, in summer and autumn; up to 25cm (10in). Sunny position in any good garden soil. Propagate by division.

Sorbus (Rosaceae) ○
One hundred species of trees and shrubs from the northern hemisphere of which one, *S. reducta,* is grown in the rock garden. White flowers in summer, with autumn berries; 30cm (12in) high. Sunny well-drained position. Propagate by cuttings.

Spiraea (Rosaceae) ○☆
Large genus of shrubs with a few for the rock garden. White or pink flowers; summer flowering; up to 30cm (12in). Sunny well-drained position. Propagate by cuttings.

Spiranthes (Orchidaceae) Ladies' Tresses ○▲
Small genus of terrestrial orchids with spirally arranged flowers. White flowers; summer and autumn flowering; up to 15cm (6in). Sunny well-drained position. Propagate by division.

Stachys (Labiatae) ○
Large genus of which most are unsuitable for the rock garden; several, however, are grown. Pink or purple flowers in summer; up to 30cm (12in). Sunny well-drained position. Propagate by division.

Stellera (Thymaelaceae) ○▲
Small genus usually represented by *S. chamaejasme* from the Himalaya to China. White flowers in the former location and yellow in the latter; summer flowering; 30cm (12in) high. Sunny well-drained position. Propagate by seed.

Sternbergia (Amaryllidaceae) ○
Small genus of dwarf bulbs from Europe into Asia. Crocus-like flowers, mostly yellow in colour; spring or autumn flowering; up to 15cm (6in). Sunny well-drained position; most best grown in alpine house or bulb frame. Propagate by seed or division.

Symphyandra (Campanulaceae) ○☆
Small genus from Europe into Asia of beautiful bellflowers. White, blue or purple; summer flowering; up to 30cm (12in). Sunny well-drained position. Propagate by seed; some can self-sow invasively.

Synthris (Scrophulariaceae) ◑□
Small genus from North America with spikes of blue flowers; spring flowering; up to 20cm (8in). Cool woodland conditions with lime-free soil. Suitable for the peat bed. Propagate by division.

Talinum (Portulacaceae) ○
Small genus of succulent-leaved plants related to the lewisias; some cushion-forming. White or magenta flowers; mainly summer flowering; up to 15cm (6in). Sunny well-drained position, but best given alpine house treatment. Propagate by seed.

Tanacetum (Compositae) Tansy ○
A 50 species genus from the northern hemisphere, grown mainly for their silver, aromatic foliage. Yellow or white flowers in summer; up to 30cm (12in). Sunny well-drained position; often grown in alpine house. Propagate by cuttings.

Tecophilaea (Amaryllidaceae) ○
Two species of dwarf bulbs from Chile which have died out in the wild. Blue

flowers, in one case, *T. cyanocrocus,* intense blue, crocus-shaped flowers; spring flowering; 10cm (4in) high. For the alpine house or bulb frame. Propagate by division.

Telesonix (Saxifragaceae) ◑
One species genus, *T. jamesii* (until recently named *Boykinia jamesii*) from North America. Tufted plants with spikes of rich red flowers; early summer flowering; 15cm (6in) high. Cool, woodland soil. Propagate by seed.

Teucrium (Labiatae) Germander ○
Large genus (300 species) especially from the Mediterranean region. Many suitable for the rock garden or alpine house. Aromatic foliage; pink to purple flowers; summer flowering; up to 25cm (10in). Sunny well-drained position or alpine house. Propagate by cuttings or seed.

Thalictrum (Ranunculaceae) Meadow Rue ◑
Several of this large genus suitable for the alpine garden. Elegant sprays of pink, mauve or yellow flowers; summer flowering; up to 30cm (12in). Cool, part shady position in humus-rich soil; ideal for the peat garden. Propagate by division or seed.

Thlaspi (Cruciferae) ○
Sixty species mainly from northern hemisphere, some of which are good rock garden plants. Pink, mauve or white flowers; spring and summer flowering; up to 15cm (6in). Sunny well-drained position. Propagate by seed.

Thymus (Labiatea) ○☆
Large genus (300–400 species) of aromatic shrubby plants, many suitable for the rock garden. Pink, purple or white flowers; summer flowering; up to 23cm (9in). Sunny well-drained position. Propagate by cuttings or seed.

Tiarella (Saxifragaceae) ◑
Small genus of Asian and North American plants related to the heucheras. Woodland plants with foaming sprays of white or pink flowers; summer flowering; up to 30cm (12in). Cool woodland conditions; suitable for the rock garden. Propagate by division or seed.

Tofieldia (Liliaceae) Bog Asphodel ○◑
Small genus of moisture-loving plants with white or yellow flowers; spring and summer flowering; up to 25cm (10in). Open position with moist, peaty soil; suitable for the peat garden. Propagate by division or seed.

Tolmiea (Saxifragaceae) ◑☆
Single species genus (*T. menziesii*) from North America. Grown mainly for foliage but has arching stems of greenish-yellow flowers; summer flowering; 25cm (10in) high. Woodland conditions with peaty soil; suitable for the peat garden. Propagate by division or seed.

Townsendia (Compositae) ○
Genus of 20 dwarf species from North America. Daisy- or aster-like flowers in mauve, pink or white; summer flowering; up to 15cm (6in). Sunny well-drained position. Not long-lived. Propagate by seed.

Trachelium (Campanulaceae) ○
Small genus (seven species) from the Mediterranean area. Heads of lilac or blue

flowers in summer; up to 15cm (6in). Sunny well-drained position, protected in winter, or alpine house culture. Propagate by seed.

Tricyrtis (Liliaceae) Toad Lily ◗☆
Ten species from the Far East. Strange spotted flowers in purple, white or yellow; summer and autumn flowering; up to 45cm (18in). Cool woodland conditions with peaty soil; ideal for peat garden. Propagate by division.

Trifolium (Leguminosae) Clover ○
Large genus (300 species) from around the world. Heads of pea-like flowers in pink, red, purple, yellow and white; summer flowering; up to 30cm (12in). Sunny position in any good soil. Propagate by seed or division.

Trillium (Liliaceae) Wake Robin ◗
Wonderful genus of woodland plants from North America and the Far East. Petals, sepals and leaves all in threes. White, yellow or red flowers; spring flowering; up to 35cm (14in). Cool woodland conditions with a peaty soil; ideal for peat gardens. Propagate by seed or division.

Trollius (Ranunculaceae) Globe Flower ○◗
Small genus of globular, buttercup-like, golden-yellow flowers; summer flowering; up to 30cm (12in). Open position in moisture retentive soil. Propagate by division or seed.

Tropaeolum (Tropaeolaceae) ○
Large genus of tuberous plants from Mexico and South America. Most too tender (except for alpine house) except *T. polyphyllum* which is buried deep enough to avoid the frosts. Bright flowers of red, yellow or blue; summer flowering. Sunny well-drained position. Propagate by division of rhizomes.

Tulipa (Liliaceae) ○☆
Large (100 species), well-known genus of bulbs from Europe to Central Asia. Flowers upright in a wide variety of colours; spring flowering; up to 25cm (10in). Sunny well-drained position. Some prefer alpine house or bulb frame. Propagate by seed or division.

Uvularia (Liliaceae) ◗☆
Small genus of pendent yellow woodland flowers from North America; early summer flowering. Cool, woodland soil; ideal for the rock garden. Propagate by division.

Vaccinium (Ericaceae) ○☐☆
Large (400 species) genus of shrubs, quite a number being suitable for the alpine garden. Small pink bell-shaped flowers followed by attractive berries; summer flowering; up to 30cm (12in). Open position in gritty-peaty soil; lime-hater. Propagate by cuttings.

Vancouveria (Berberidaceae) ○◗
Small genus, from North America, similar to the epimediums. Arching stems of yellow or white flowers in early summer; up to 30cm (12in). Peaty woodland conditions. Suitable for the peat garden but can be invasive. Propagate by division.

Verbascum (Scrophulariaceae) Mullein ○
Large genus (360 species) of mainly big plants; a few smaller ones suitable for the

rock garden. Yellow or pink flowers; summer and autumn flowering; up to 30cm (12in). Sunny well-drained position. Propagate by seed.

Veronica (Scrophulariaceae) ○
Large genus (300 species) of mainly blue flowers, many of which are suitable for the rock garden or alpine house. Summer flowering; up to 25cm (10in). Sunny well-drained position. Propagate by division, cuttings or seed.

Viola (Violaceae) ○◑
Well-loved genus of plants, most of which are suitable for the rock garden. Five hundred species from around the world, in a large range of colours; spring to winter flowering; up to 20cm (8in). Sunny well-drained position, but some prefer part shade and a moister soil. Propagate by seed or cuttings.

Wahlenbergia (Campanulaceae) ○
Large genus (125 species) mainly from the southern hemisphere. Similar to *Edrianthus* with blue or pink flowers; summer flowering; up to 7.5cm (3in). Sunny well-drained position. Propagate by seed or cuttings.

Waldsteinia (Rosaceae) ○◑☆
Small genus from northern hemisphere. Yellow flowers similar to potentilla; summer flowering; up to 20cm (8in). Sunny or part shady position in any good garden soil. Propagate by division; can be invasive.

Woodsia (Polypodiaceae) ◑
Wide-ranging genus (40 species) of small ferns suitable for the rock garden; up to 25cm (10in). Cool moist position; particularly likes north-facing crevices. Propagate by spores.

Wulfenia (Scrophulariaceae) ○
Small genus from Europe and the Himalaya. Spikes of purple flowers in summer; up to 30cm (12in). Sunny well-drained but moisture retentive position. Propagate by seed.

Zauschneria (Onagraceae) ○
Small genus of subshrubby plants from North America. Red tubular flower in summer; up to 30cm (12in). Warm sunny position with well-drained soil. Propagate by cuttings.

Zephyranthes (Amaryllidaceae) ○☆
Genus of South American bulbs of which one, *Z. candida,* is grown in the rock garden. White crocus-shaped flowers; autumn flowering; 15cm (6in) high. Warm sunny position with a gritty-peaty soil. Propagate by division.

Appendix I Plant Lists

Plants for troughs and sinks

Aethionema species
Anacyclus depressus
Androsace jaquemontii
Androsace sempervivoides
Androsace villosa
Antennaria dioica 'Minima'
Aquilegia species
Arenaria tetraquetra
Asperula nitida
Campanula species
Convolvulus nitida
Daphne species
Dianthus species
Douglasia species
Draba species
Dryas octopetala 'Minor'
Erigeron species
Erinus alpinus
Genista delphinensis
Gentiana species
Geranium farreri
Geum reptans
Gypsophila aretioides
Gypsophila repens
Helichrysum milfordiae
Iris reticulata group
Juniperus communis 'Compressa'
Lewisia species
Linaria alpina
Micromeria species
Myosotis species
Penstemon species
Petrocallis pyrenaica
Petrophytum caespitosum
Phlox species
Physoplexis comosa
Polygala species
Potentilla verna nana
Primula species

Raoulia species
Salix boydii
Salix serpyllifolia
Saponaria species
Saxifraga species
Sedum species
Sempervivum species
Silene acaulis
Soldanella species
Thlaspi species
Thymus species
Veronica species
Vitaliana primuliflora
Wahlenbergia species

Plants for tufa

Androsace species
Arenaria tetraquetra
Asperula suberosa
Campanula species
Douglasia species
Draba species
Edrianthus pumilo
Erinus alpinus
Eritricium nanum
Lewisia species
Myosotis rupicola
Petrocallis pyrenaica
Petrophytum caespitosum
Physoplexis comosa
Saxifraga species
Vitaliana primuliflora

Plants for walls

Achillea species
Aethionema species
Alyssum saxatile
Arabis species
Asarina procumbens
Asplenium species (shade)

Aubrieta deltoidea
Blechnum species (shade)
Campanula species
Chiastophyllum oppositifolium (shade)
Convolvulus sabatius
Corydalis lutea (shade)
Dianthus species
Erinus alpinus
Erodium species
Gypsophila species
Haberlea rhodopensis (shade)
Helianthemum
Iberis sempervirens
Linaria alpina
Linaria cymbalaria (shade)
Onosma species
Phlox douglasii
Phlox subulata
Polygonum affine
Polypodium species (shade)
Ramonda species (shade)
Saponaria ocymoides
Saxifraga species (some shade)
Sedum species
Sempervivum species
Thymus species
Zauschneria californica

Plants for peat beds (moist shade)

Aconitum species
Adiatum species
Adonis species
Andromeda
Anemone species
Anemonella species
Arctostaphylos uva-ursi
Arisaema species
Arisarum proboscideum
Arum species
Astilbe species
Bletilla striata
Calceolaria species
Caltha species
Cardamine species
Cassiope species
Clintonia species
Convallaria species
Coptis species
Cornus species

Cortusa species
Corydalis cashmeriana
Cypripedium species
Dodecatheon species
Epigeae species
Epimedium species
Epipactis species
Eranthis species
Erythronium species
Galanthus species
Gaultheria species
Gentiana species
Glaucidium palmatum
Haberlea species
Hacquetia epipactis
Helleborus species
Hepatica species
Hosta species
Houstonia caerulea
Hylomecon japonicum
Hypsela species
Isopyrum thalictrioides
Jeffersonia dubia
Kalmiopsis leachiana
Ledum species
Linnaea borealis
Lithophragma parviflora
Meconopsis species
Mertensia species
Mimulus species
Mitella species
Omphalagrama species
Ourisia species
Parnassia species
Pernettya species
Phyllodoce species
Pleione formosana
Polygonatum species
Pratia species
Primula species
Pyrola species
Rhododendron species
Rhodohypoxis species
Sanguinaria canadensis
Scoliopus species
Shortia species
Soldanella species
Synthris species
Thalictrum species

Tofieldia species
Tolmiea menziesii
Tricyrtis species
Trillium species
Vaccinium species
Vancouveria species

Plants for the bulb frame

Calochortus species
Colchicum species
Corydalis species
Crocus species
Cyclamen species
Fritillaria species
Habranthus species
Hippeastrum species
Ipheion species
Iris species
Leucojum species
Lilium species
Merendera species
Muscari species
Narcissus species
Ranunculus asiaticus
Romulea species
Scilla species
Sternbergia species
Tecophilea species
Tulipa species

Plants for alpine lawns

Acaena species

Arenaria species
Campanula creeping species
Cotula species
Hutchinsonia alpina
Hypericum prostrate species
Hypsela longiflora
Linaria species
Nierembergia rivularis
Pratia species
Sedum species
Thymus species

Plants for waterside situations

Astilbe chinensis
Caltha palustris
Cardamine pratensis 'Flore Pleno'
Gentiana species
Epipactis palustris
Fritillaria meleagris
Iris species
Leucojum aestivum
Lysimachia nummularia
Mazus species
Mimulus species
Myosotis species
Parnassia palustris
Pinguicula species
Primula species
Ranunculus species
Plus many of the peat garden plants

Appendix II Bibliography

Alpine Garden Society, *Alpine Gardening* (periodical), 1986–
Alpine Garden Society, *Quarterly Bulletin* (periodical), 1930–
American Rock Garden Society, *Rocky Mountain Alpines,* Timber Press, 1986
Bacon, L., *Mountain Flower Holidays in Europe,* Alpine Garden Society, 1979
Bawden, H. E., *Dwarf Shrubs,* Alpine Garden Society, 1980
Brickell C. D. & Mathew, B., *Daphne,* Alpine Garden Society, 1976
Cribb, P. & Butterfield, I., *The Genus Pleione,* Christopher Helm, 1988
Davis, P. *et al., Wild Orchids of Britain and Europe,* Chatto & Windus, 1983
Dryden, K., *Alpines in Pots,* Alpine Garden Society, 1988
Elliott, J., *Alpines in Sinks and Troughs,* Alpine Garden Society, 1975
Elliott, R., *Alpine Gardening,* Alpine Garden Society, reprinted 1988
Gledhill, D., *The Names of Plants,* Cambridge University Press, 1985
Good, J., *Handbook of Rock Gardening,* Alpine Garden Society, 1988
Grey-Wilson, C., *The Alpine Flowers of Britain and Europe,* Collins, 1979
Grey-Wilson, C., *The Genus Cyclamen,* Christopher Helm, 1988
Grey-Wilson, C., *Dionysia,* Alpine Garden Society, 1989
Grey-Wilson, C. (ed.), *A Manual of Alpine and Rock Garden Plants,* Christopher
    Helm, 1989
Griffith, A., *Collins Guide to Alpines and Rock Garden Plants,* Collins, 1973
Hulme, J. K., *Propagation of Alpine Plants,* Alpine Garden Society, 1982
Huxley, A., *Mountain Flowers of Europe,* Blandford, 1973
Ingwersen, W., *Alpine & Rock Plants,* Dent, 1983
Ingwersen, W., *Manual of Alpine Plants,* Ingwersen, 1978
Mathew, B., *The Iris,* Batsford, 1981
Mathew, B., *The Crocus,* Batsford, 1982
Mathew, B., *The Smaller Bulbs,* Batsford, 1987
Plant Finder, Hardy Plant Society/Headmain, annual
Polunin, O., *Flowers of Greece and the Balkans,* Oxford University Press, 1980
Polunin, O. & Stainton, A., *Flowers of the Himalaya,* Oxford University Press,
    1984
Rix, M. & Philips, R., *The Bulb Book,* Pan Books, 1981
Smith, G. F. & Lowe, D., *Androsace,* Alpine Garden Society, 1977
Smith, G. F. *et al., Primulas of Europe and America,* Alpine Garden Society, 1984
Webb, D. A. & Gornall, R. J., *Saxifrages of Europe,* Christopher Helm, 1989
Yeo, P., *Hardy Geraniums,* Christopher Helm, 1985

Appendix III Societies and Suppliers

Societies

Alpine Garden Society, The Secretary, Lye End Link, St John's, Woking, Surrey GU21 1SW

American Rock Garden Society, The Secretary, 15 Fairmead Road, Darien, Connecticut 06820, USA

New Zealand Alpine Garden Society, The Secretary, 17 Courage Road, Amberley, New Zealand

Scottish Rock Garden Club, The Secretary, 21 Erchiston Park, Edinburgh EH10 4PW

Vancouver Island Rock and Alpine Garden Society, The Secretary, PO Box 6507, Station C, Victoria, BC V8P 5M4, Canada

Suppliers

Great Britain

Cambridge Bulbs, (Norman Stevens), 40 Whittlesford Road, Newton, Cambridge CB2 5PH

Holden Clough Nursery, (Peter Foley), Bolton-by-Bowland, Clitheroe, Lancashire

Ingwersens, Birch Farm Nursery, Gravetye, East Grinstead, West Sussex RH19 4LE

Inshriach Alpine Plant Nursery, (Jack Drake), Aviemore, Inverness-shire PH22 1QS

Lismore Alpines, (Brian & Judy Burrows), Sandy Hill, Low Bentham Road, High Bentham, Via Lancaster, North Yorkshire LA2 7BS

Oakdene Alpine Plant Nursery, (David Sampson), Oakdene, Scotsford Road, Broad Oak, Heathfield, East Sussex TN21 8TU

R. F. Beeston, 294 Ombersley Road, Worcester WR3 7HD

Potterton & Martin, The Cottage Nursery, Moortown Road, Nettleton, Nr. Castor, North Lincolnshire LN7 6HX

Tile Barn Nursery, (Peter Moore), Standen Street, Iden Green, Benenden, Kent TN17 4LB

United States

Colorado Alpines Inc., PO Box 2708, Avon, CO 81620

Lamb's Nurseries, E.101 Sharp Avenue, Spokane, Washington 99202

Mt Tahoma Nursery, 28111-112th Avenue East, Graham, Washington 98338

Oliver Nurseries Inc., 1159 Bronson Road, Fairfield, CT 06430

Rice Creek Gardens Inc., 1315 66th Avenue Northeast, Minneapolis, Minnesota 55432

Rocknoll Nursery, 9210 US 50, Hillsboro, Ohio 45133-8546

Rocky Mountain Rare Plants, PO Box 20483, Denver, CO 80220-0483

Russell Graham, 4030 Eagle Crest Road Northwest, Salem, Oregon 97304

Siskiyou Rare Plant Nursery, 2825 Cummings Road, Medford, Oregon 97501

Index

Page numbers in *italic* refer to the line illustrations